"I SMILED AT MYSELF AT THE SIGHT OF ALL THIS MONEY. 'OH, DRUG,' SAID
I, ALOUD, 'WHAT ART THOU GOOD FOR? THOU ART NOT WORTH TO ME,
NO, NOT THE TAKING OFF THE GROUND. ONE OF THESE KNIVES IS
WORTH ALL THIS HEAP.'"—*Page* 9.

ROBINSON CRUSOE'S MONEY;

OR, THE

REMARKABLE FINANCIAL FORTUNES AND MISFORTUNES OF A REMOTE ISLAND COMMUNITY.

By DAVID A. WELLS,

LATE U. S. SPECIAL COMMISSIONER OF REVENUE.

WITH ILLUSTRATIONS BY THOMAS NAST.

"It requires a great deal of philosophy to observe once what may be seen every day."—ROUSSEAU.

NEW YORK
PETER SMITH
1931

PREFACE.

THE origin of this little book is as follows: Some months ago, the expediency was suggested to the author, by certain prominent friends of hard money in this country, of preparing for popular reading—and possibly for political campaign purposes—a little tract, or essay, in which the elementary principles underlying the important subjects of money and currency should be presented and illustrated from the simplest A B C stand-point. That such a work was desirable, and that none of the very great number of speeches and essays already published on these topics in all respects answered the existing requirement, was admitted; but how to invest subjects, so often discussed, and so commonly regarded as dry and abstract, with sufficient new interest to render them at once attractive and intelligible to those whose tastes disincline them to close reasoning and investigation, was a matter not easy to determine.

At last the old idea—recognized in fables, allegories, and parables—of making a story the medium for communicating instruction, suggested itself; and, in accordance with the suggestion, a remote island community has been imagined, in which, starting from conditions but one remove from barbarism, but gradually rising to a high degree of civilization, the progress, the use, and the abuse of the instrumentalities and mechanism of exchange—through barter, money, and currency—have been traced consecutively; and the effect of the application of not a few of the most popular fiscal recommendations and theories of the day practically worked out and recorded. And, in carrying out this scheme, the reader will not fail to perceive, by reference to the marginal notes accompanying the text, that hardly an absurdity in reference to exchange, money, or currency can be imagined, which somewhere and at some time has not had its exact counterpart in actual history or experience.

If any apology for the objects designed or the course pursued is needed, the author thinks he finds it in the precedent established by the illustrious Geoffrey Crayon, Gent., who, in the introduction to his " Tales of a Traveler," thus happily sets forth the special advantage which accrues from the proper employment of a story as a means of communicating information. " I am not," he says, " for those barefaced tales which carry their moral on their surface, staring one in the face; on the contrary, I have often hid my moral from sight, and disguised it as much as possible by sweets and spices; so that while the simple reader is listening with open mouth to a ghost or love story, he may have a bolus of sound morality popped down his throat, and be never the wiser for the fraud."

Whether in " Robinson Crusoe's Money " the author shall succeed in inducing his fellow-countrymen—to whom the ordinary currency medicine is becoming distasteful—to swallow without wry faces the same dose sugar-coated, remains to be determined.

NORWICH, Conn., *January*, 1876.

CONTENTS.

8   *CONTENTS.*

ILLUSTRATIONS.

ROBINSON CRUSOE'S MONEY.

CHAPTER I.

THE THREE GREAT BAGS OF MONEY.

ALL who have read " Robinson Crusoe" (and who has not?) will remember the circumstance of his opening, some time after he had become domiciled on his desolate island, one of the chests that had come to him from the ship. In it he found pins, needles and thread, a pair of large scissors, " ten or a dozen good knives," some cloth, about a dozen and a half of white linen handkerchiefs concerning which he remarks, " They were exceedingly refreshing to wipe my face on a warm day ;" and, finally, hidden away in the till of the chest, " *three great bags of money*—gold as well as silver."

The finding of all these articles—the money excepted—it will be further remembered, greatly delighted the heart of Crusoe; inasmuch as they increased his store of useful things, and therefore increased his comfort and happiness. But in respect to the money the case was entirely different. It was a thing to him, under the circumstances, absolutely worthless, and over its presence and finding he soliloquized as follows: " I smiled at myself at the sight of all this money. 'Oh, drug!' said I, aloud, 'what art thou good for? Thou art not worth to me, no, not the taking off the ground. One of these knives is worth all this heap. Nay, I would give it all for a gross of tobacco-pipes; for sixpenny-worth of turnip and carrot seed from England; or for a handful of pease and beans, and a bottle of ink.'"

In introducing this episode in the life of his hero, nothing was probably further from the thought of the author, De Foe, than the intent to give his readers a lesson in political economy. And yet it would be difficult to find an illustration which conveys in so simple a manner to him who reflects upon it so much of information in respect to the nature of that which is popularly termed "*wealth;*" or so good a basis for reasoning correctly in respect to the origin and function of that which we call "*money.*" And in such reasoning, the truth of the following propositions is too evident to require demonstration:

1st. The pins and needles, the scissors, knives, and cloth were of great *utility* to Robinson Crusoe, because their possession satisfied a great desire on his part to have them, and greatly increased his comfort and happiness.

2d. Possessing utility, they nevertheless possessed no exchangeable *value*, because they could not be bought or sold, or, what is the same thing, exchanged with any body for any thing.

3d. They had, moreover, no *price*, for they had no purchasing power which could be expressed as money.

4th. The money, which is popularly regarded as the symbol and the concentration of all wealth, had, under the circumstances, neither utility, value, nor price. It could not be eaten, drunk, worn, used as a tool, or exchanged with any body for any thing, and fully merited the appellation which Crusoe in another place gives it, of "*sorry, worthless stuff.*"

Finally, the pins, needles, knives, cloth, and scissors were all *capital* to Robinson Crusoe, because they were all instrumentalities capable of being used to produce something additional, to him useful or desirable. The money was *not capital*, under the circumstances, because it could not be used to produce any thing.

Starting, then, with a condition of things on the island in which money had clearly neither utility nor value, let us next consider under what change of domestic circumstances it could become useful, acquire value, become an object of exchange, and constitute a standard for establishing prices.

CHAPTER II.

A NEW SOCIAL ORDER OF THINGS.

THE first person that came to join Robinson Crusoe on his island was Friday, and next, Friday's father. But even with this increase of numbers there was still no use for the money, inasmuch as the three constituted but one family, the members of which labored and shared all useful things they acquired in common, and made no exchanges. But when Will Atkins and the English sailors came, and the population of the island, we may suppose, was largely and permanently increased, a new social order of things became inevitable. Incompatibility of taste and temper, and a natural desire for personal independence, soon made it impossible for all to live and share in common as one family. And self-interest also soon taught, that, in order that the quantity of useful things available for the new community as a whole might be increased, and their quality perfected, it was desirable, that, instead of each man endeavoring to supply all his own wants,

and for this purpose following irregularly the business of a
carpenter, baker, tailor, mason, and the like, it was best for
each man to pursue but one occupation, and, making himself
skilled in it, procure the things which he himself did not produce, and which he might need, by exchanging his own products or services for the products or services of some other
man.   They saw instinctively that Robinson Crusoe, although
originally civilized, would, if he had remained alone on the
island, have inevitably become a pure savage, and simply
because he was alone, and could make no exchanges.   For
a time, the things which he obtained from the wreck raised
him above this condition; for what the ship brought him—the
knives, axes, guns, cloth, etc.—were capital, or the accumulated
labor of other men.   But if the ship had given him nothing,
he would have had to make every thing for himself—"his
hat, his garments, his feet-covering, his bread, his meat with
bow and arrows, his house by blows of his hatchet, his hatchet
by blows of his hammer, his hammer heaven knows how"—
and become a barbarian in spite of himself, because all his
effort would have been required, and would have only sufficed,
to insure him a bare subsistence.

Systematic division of labor and the exchange of products
and services thus, for the first time on the island, came in, and
constituted a part of the perfected machinery of production,
or the means of getting a living.   And it is also to be here
noted, that, because commodities and services now for the first
time became exchangeable, they also for the first time acquired
the attribute which we call *value.*

CHAPTER III.

THE PERIOD OF BARTER.

ALL exchanges must, however, in the first instance, have been made directly, or, as we term it, by *barter;* so much of one commodity or service being given for so much of some other commodity or service—corn for cloth, furs and skins for knives or tobacco, so much labor in building a house for so much skill in constructing a canoe. But in all this method of exchanging, which, while it is the most ancient, is also one which still extensively prevails in even the most civilized societies, there was no place for the use or intervention of money; and consequently, also, there was no such thing as price; for price, as before stated, is the purchasing power of any commodity or service expressed in money.

But the people on Robinson Crusoe Island soon found out by experience that there was an obstacle in the way of carrying on all exchanges according to the principle of direct barter, so serious in its nature as to constitute, unless removed, a complete bar to any further considerable progress in civilization and social development. And the discovery happened somewhat in this wise:

Twist, who was a tailor, and had made a coat, discovered all at once that he was out of bread; and being hungry, suspended work, and went in search of Needum, the baker, to effect an exchange. He found him without difficulty, just heating his oven, and with plenty of bread to dispose of; but as the baker had all the coats he wanted, he declined to trade.

Needum, however, kindly informed Twist that if any fellow should call with any surplus grain or flour, he (Needum) would be most happy to supply him with all the bread he needed in exchange; but as the tailor was neither a farmer nor a miller, and had neither of these articles, he (Twist) set off for the other end of the island, where there was another baker, to see how the latter was situated in respect to garments. On his way, Twist was overtaken by Pecks, the mason, who had no coat, and, wanting the very garment which Twist had been making, had stopped work on a stone wall and gone in search of the tailor, to whom he proposed to exchange the coat for a new chimney. But as Twist had already two chimneys to his house, and nothing to cook, and didn't want another chimney, the mason was as unsuccessful in his effort to trade with the tailor as the tailor had been just before with the baker. At last, after much vexatious traveling about, involving great waste of time and labor, Twist found a baker who wanted to exchange bread for the coat, and Pecks a tailor who would give a coat for a chimney; Needum having, in the mean time, shut up his bakery and gone in search of Diggs, the farmer, who was willing to supply grain for bread. But when all these different persons, each desirous of exchanging his special products or services, had been found, and had come together, a new perplexity at once made its appearance, and one so embarrassing as to cause each man seriously to consider whether it were not better to return home and endeavor to produce every thing for himself, rather than attempt to exchange any thing. "For how," said they all, "is the comparative value of our different commodities and services which we propose to exchange to be ascertained?" "How can I know," said Twist, "how many loaves I ought to receive for my coat?" "Or I," said Pecks, "find out how high and broad a chimney I ought

to make for my garment?" Diggs, furthermore, got up a little private dispute of his own with Needum, growing out of
the circumstance that the latter wanted to make his entire
payment in bread to the former at once; while Diggs, who
did not relish the idea of living on stale and possibly moldy
bread for an indefinite length of time, wanted pay for his
grain, from the baker, at the rate of one fresh loaf per day.
As for poor Twist, he had become by this time so humble
through hunger that he had not the heart to object to the
proposition to take a cart-load of bread at once in exchange
for his coat, although his house was so small that he knew he
would have to store part of his "pay" on the roof, where it
would be certain to be eaten by others than his own family.

There was another incident which happened about this
time which made much talk among the island community.
A man who had nothing to sell but his labor had been employed to load a vessel with coal—a vein of which had been
discovered; and, after working faithfully all day, had received
in pay for his services a ton of coal. But as it was meat,
drink, and lodging, and not coal (although the latter was greatly needed for some purposes), which the laborer wanted, there
was nothing left for the laborer to do but to attempt to exchange his coal, and that, too, as soon as possible, in order to
satisfy his immediate necessities. Being too poor to hire a
horse and cart, he therefore borrowed a wheelbarrow, and, filling it with coal, went in search of persons who had a surplus
of meat, drink, and lodgings to dispose of. But all of them
happened to have all the coal they wanted; and morning
found the laborer still trundling through the streets his most
useful commodity unexchanged, and ready to sink with hunger
and exposure. A like experience befell also the journeyman
butcher, blacksmith, carpenter, and dry-goods clerk, who re-

2

ceived for their day's labor respectively a sheep-skin, a dozen
horse-shoes, a piece of pine timber, and two yards of red flan-
nel.   All were in no condition, through bodily exhaustion, to
resume work on the next day; and all also clearly saw that
their condition would not have been much improved, if each
had received an entire payment in either meat, drink, or lodg
ing, in place of coal, skin, lumber, horseshoes, or cloth.

THE REPRESENTATIVES OF LABOR AND THE REPRESENTATIVES OF CAPITAL
PROPOSING TO HAVE A DIFFERENCE.

The laborers, therefore, held a meeting, and at once resolved : "That whereas it was evident that the system of paying for labor with a portion of the commodity which each laborer produced would necessitate as much time and labor to make their wages serviceable to their wants as was required in the first instance to earn said wages; therefore, it was but right and proper that the employers should allow the laborers to use half of the whole time for which they were paid, for the purpose of rendering their wages wholly available for their immediate necessities." But to this the employers rejoined that such an agreement would be equivalent not only to doubling the proportion of wages to direct production, but also to impairing, to the extent of one-half, the effectiveness of all labor engaged in production, thereby increasing scarcity, diminishing abundance, and rendering further advance in material development exceedingly slow, if not altogether impossible. For a time, therefore, there was a prospect of a very serious difficulty between the representatives of labor and the representatives of capital ; resulting, as is always the case, in immense losses, not only to those directly concerned, but to the whole community.

CHAPTER IV.

HOW THEY INVENTED MONEY.

THE people on the island—both laborers and employers—
were, however, fully agreed that life was too short to waste
a good part of it in a game of "blindman's-buff" on a large
scale—for such this attempt to conduct exchanges on a basis
of direct barter substantially was ;* but they nevertheless also
clearly perceived that the game would continue to be played,
to the interruption of all material progress, unless some other
method of exchanging could be devised and adopted.   Under
the guidance, therefore, as it were, of instinct (Robinson Crusoe encouraging), *and without any enactment of law,* Twist,
Needum, Pecks, Diggs, Friday, Friday's father, Will Atkins,
and every body else, by common consent, agreed to select and

---

* That the inconveniences experienced by a community attempting to
conduct its exchanges exclusively by pure and direct barter as here depict-
ed, are not only not imaginary, but have their exact counterpart in the
present every-day experiences of countries of great geographical area and
population, is proved by the testimony of Barth, Burton, and other recent
travelers in Eastern Africa.   Thus Barth, for example, says (see "Travels,"
vol. i., p. 568; vol. iii., p. 203) that he was repeatedly prevented from buying
what he absolutely needed—corn, rice, etc.—because he did not have, and
could not get, what the people wanted in exchange ; and, again (vol. ii., p.
51), he states that so great was the difficulty of getting things in some of
the African towns which he visited, in consequence of the people having
no general medium of exchange, that his servants would often return from
their purchasing expeditions in a state of the utmost exhaustion.

adopt some single commodity which all should agree to take in exchange for whatever of products or services they might have to dispose of; so that whenever any one had any thing to exchange, he might first exchange it for this commodity, whatever it might be, and then with such *intermediate object* purchase at such times and places, and in such proportions as he might desire, whatever he might need. And the moment this was done, civilization on the island took a long step forward, and the first great embarrassment growing out of the attempt to exchange exclusively by direct barter was removed. The tailor was no longer in danger of starving; the mason had no longer any anxiety about procuring clothing, and the laborer received as pay for his labor something which gave him an equivalent in meat, drink, lodging, and other necessities which he might need, without trouble; every man giving freely of his goods or services for the intermediate object, because he knew that every other person desirous of exchanging would be willing to do the same.

Again: the selection of some commodity or article, and the investing it by common consent with a universal and comparatively unvarying purchasing power, also solved the second perplexity, inasmuch as it provided a measure or standard, for ascertaining the comparative value or purchasing power of every other exchangeable commodity or service; and in precisely the same manner as the length or weight of any thing is ascertained, *i. e.*, by comparing it with some other thing which the community have universally agreed to recognize as a standard of length or weight—as, for example, the rod of wood which we call a yard-stick, or a piece of metal which is termed a pound. "My loaves are each worth ten pieces of the intermediate commodity," said Needum, the baker! "My coat," rejoined Twist, the tailor, "is worth a thousand pieces!" The terms of fair exchange between the baker and the tailor would therefore have been one hundred loaves for one coat.

The general name given to the *commodities* or *articles* which the people of different countries universally accept in exchange, as the equivalent for all other commodities or services, and as the measure of values, is *money*.

The commodities or articles which have been selected by men at various times and places to serve as this universal equivalent, intermediate agent, or medium for facilitating exchanges, have been exceedingly various. Among the North American Indians, and the early settlers who came among them, wampum and beaver-skins were used as money; among the natives of West Africa, money consists of small shells called " cowries;" in Abyssinia, the common money of to-day is salt; in Chinese Tartary, it is cubes of pressed tea; and within a comparatively recent period small cakes of soap have been used as money on the west coast of Mexico. Among pastoral people of antiquity, cattle and sheep were so extensively used for money that our common English word *pecuniary* has its derivation from the old word *pecus*, signifying a flock. And while we read in Homer that the price of the armor of Glaucus was one hundred head of cattle, we also know that the Zulus of South Africa pay their debts to-day in cattle, and reckon their wealth by the same standard.

Money, therefore, existed before statutes, and exists and is used to-day among nations who have no written or acknowledged code of laws.

It is also of importance to a clear understanding of this subject to recognize at this point another fundamental fact, namely, that there is no evidence that any nation or people has ever adopted, in the first instance, any article or commodity to use as money which did not possess, by reason of some inherent or intrinsic desirable qualities, a natural purchasing power or value. And a little reflection will make it obvious that this must have been so from necessity. For in the absence of all law defining what money should be, and regulating exchanges, the adoption of any article to serve as money which represented little or no effort for its production or accumulation would enable the shrewd, the idle, or unscrupulous, easily, and without fear of punishment or restraint, to take from the rest of the community products which represented the expenditure of time and labor, without giving in return any equivalent. Thus, for example, if dried leaves, or pieces of paper with such marks as any might choose to stamp or scrawl upon them, had been invested with a universal purchasing power, the primary practical result of the use of such money would have been to enable somebody to obtain something for nothing, or to permit those who would not work or save, to rob those who did. The people on the island, being uneducated, never did any such foolish thing; but when they came to study history, they found out, to their great surprise, that the people of other countries had repeatedly used things worthless in themselves as money; and many years afterward a man who aspired to be a great teacher even came to the island from the United States, and endeavored to convince the people that it was a great defect to use any thing as money which had any intrinsic value as a commodity.* The

---

* "The precious metals have many qualities which fit them for use as

children of the first school he attempted to talk to soon made
his position embarrassing by reading from their histories that
the people of every country, especially the poor and ill-informed, who had ever attempted to facilitate their exchanges
by using something as money which had no intrinsic value,
had in every case been so swindled and robbed, as a consequence, that sooner or later they were always compelled, as a
measure of simple self-protection, to abandon its use, and in
its place adopt something as money which had a generally acknowledged and comparatively permanent inherent value or
purchasing power as a commodity.

The following were some of the narrations which the children found and read out of their histories:

"In December, 1861, a poor soldier's widow put into the savings-bank
two hundred dollars in specie, and then removed with four young children
to California.   In July, 1864, when gold stood at two hundred and eighty,
she sent for her money.   In return, she received a gold draft for eighty-
three, accrued interest at six per cent. included."—HENRY BRONSON, *Nature and Office of Money.*

"The morals of the people were corrupted (by the Continental irredeemable money) beyond any thing that could have been believed prior to the
event.   All ties of honor, blood, gratitude, humanity, and justice were dis-
solved.   Old debts were paid when the paper money was worth no more
than seventy for one.   Brothers defrauded brothers, children parents, and

coin money.   Their defects are their weight, their intrinsic value as commodities."—*Social Science and National Economy, by R. E. Thompson,* Philadelphia, 1875.

"The moment it is perceived that money is nothing but a token, it becomes evident that any token currently accepted in exchange of useful
services and products of labor will perform the proper functions of money
without regard to the material of which it is made; and that the less costly the material out of which money is made, the better for the community
that uses it."—*Money, Currency, and Banking, by Charles Moran,* New York,
1875, p. 42.

parents children. Widows, orphans, and others were paid for money lent in specie with depreciated paper."—BRECK, *Sketch of Continental Money.*

" The assignats gradually dwindled down to nothing, involving the whole land in ruin—excepting a few lucky speculators—and resulted eventually in national bankruptcy. When thousands of wretches, even before the final collapse of the assignats, were committing suicide to escape starvation, war was a blessing; and Napoleon was the instrument by means of which all Europe was made to feel the results of worthless money, either directly or by inoculation, from its maddened victims."—*Notes on the French Assignats, and their Influence.*

" He had to pay four hundred dollars for a hat; for a pair of boots the same. He wanted a good horse, but was asked a price equivalent to ten years' pay." "My six months' earnings will scarce defray the most indispensable outlay of a single day. * * * For a bed, supper, and grog for myself, my three companions, and their servants, I was charged, on going off without a breakfast next day, the sum of eight hundred and fifty dollars."—*Life of General De Kalb.*

" In all, from first to last (1835 to 1841), the amount of notes, bills, drafts, bonds, etc., issued by the Treasury of the Republic of Texas, and serving to a greater or less extent as a 'circulating medium,' amounted to $13,318,145, or at the rate of more than two hundred and sixty dollars per head of the entire population. If paper issues serving as money could have made a people rich, the Texans ought to have been the richest people in the universe. In January, 1839, Texas treasury-notes were worth no more than *forty cents on the dollar;* in the spring of 1839, they were worth thirty-seven and a half cents; in 1841, from twelve to fifteen cents; and in 1842 it required, in the characteristic language of the times, 'fifteen dollars in treasury-notes to buy three glasses of brandy-and-water without sugar.' 'By this time there was little circulating medium of any kind in Texas; but this was no great calamity, as the people had but little left to circulate.' The evils the system did were immense, and such as for which, even were it so disposed, the Government cóuld afford no compensation to the sufferers."—GOUGE'S *Fiscal History of Texas.*

Again, one of the principal objects for which money was devised and brought into use was to serve as a measure, or standard, for estimating the comparative value of other things.

But it seems hardly possible to conceive of a person desirous of using money for such purpose, selecting an article to measure values which in itself possesses no value, or costs no labor to produce, any more than he would select as a standard for measuring length something which had no length, or as a standard for measuring weight something which had no weight. The people of the island must have been unusually stupid if they did not from the outset, therefore, clearly see that nothing can be reliable and good money under all circumstances which does not of itself possess the full amount of the value which it professes on its face to possess.

----•- -

CHAPTER V.

HOW THE PEOPLE ON THE ISLAND AND ELSEWHERE LEARNED WISDOM.

But while any commodity possessed of acknowledged purchasing power or value may be used as money, the experience of the islanders and every other people must have soon taught them that some commodities are much better adapted to this purpose than others; or, rather, that the use of certain commodities as money, while they may answer the purpose, nevertheless entail very serious disadvantages. And the details of the manner in which this information has been acquired by experience constitute one of the most interesting chapters in the world's history. The experience of the islanders was somewhat as follows:

At the outset they agreed to use cowries—a pretty shell picked up on the beach, and which the women all desired to have and use as an ornament. These shells were not, however, plentiful; and, in fact, it was found that it required about as much time and labor for a man to collect a hundred of them as it did to grow a bushel of wheat. Consequently, wheat regularly exchanged for cowries (as money) at the rate of one hundred cowries for one bushel, while the farmer with two thousand cowries could readily buy a plow, which was considered equivalent in value to twenty bushels. By-and-by, some idle fellows that were in the habit of sailing made a long excursion, and, for the first time, visited a little island on the remote horizon. When they landed, they found, to their surprise, that instead of cowries being very scarce on the beach, they were very abundant. They winked at one another, and said little; but each man proceeded to gather all the cowries he could, and, returning to the main island, kept their discovery a profound secret.

The first thing of note that next happened among the Robinson Crusoe people was a great and unexpected revival in business. Money began to grow abundant. Societary circulation was never so active. Every thing that was offered for sale speedily found a purchaser, and, demand increasing, prices rapidly increased also. It was also noticed that a few persons who never did any regular work, but speculated and gambled all the morning, and took pleasant sailing excursions every afternoon, had, especially, plenty of money, which, as patriotic citizens, desirous of making trade lively, they were always most ready to part with for other commodities. The shop-keepers, the farmers, and the mechanics, all also finding that they had more money than usual, all also felt impelled to buy something, and prices took a fresh start upward, so that a bushel of wheat that could previously have been sold for one hundred cowries easily brought one hundred and fifty, and even two hundred But, on the other hand, the farmer, instead of being able to buy, as before, a plow for two thousand cowries, now found that he had to pay double, or four thousand; or, in other words, the cowries had only about one-half the purchasing power they possessed before.

But for a time every body was jubilant. Was it not evident that the value of every man's possessions, measured in cowry money, had greatly increased—and what could be more natural than that the shrewd adventurers who had been the authors of these golden days should be highly honored, invited to speak before cowry clubs in all parts of the island, and be even talked of for the chief offices, which still continued to be filled by Robinson Crusoe and his man Friday? The continually augmenting prices—measured in cowry money—of all commodities, or, what is the same thing, the continually diminishing purchasing power of the cowries, at last began to attract attention, and this in turn induced distrust; so that the price of a bushel of wheat, which had been at first one hundred cowries, and then two hundred, rose to three, four, and even five hundred cowries. Another remarkable circumstance noticed was, that, as prices increased, the wants of trade for cowry money also increased proportionably, which want the adventurers who had been the means of giving the island its increased volume of money took care to supply by bringing additional quantities of cowries as they were needed. It was also observed that, as distrust increased, there was also a remarkable increase in societary activity; for every body desired to change off his cowry money for something else.* Per-

---

* "To my mind, the great and immediate need of the day is the issuance of more legal-tender notes, in order to impair the confidence in them to an extent as to cause the owners of them to desire to exchange them for other kinds of property, or man's wants—not simply to loan out on short or long date paper, with fire-proof security, at low or high

THEN THE BUBBLE BURST; STOCK COMPANIES ALL FAILED.

sons who were in debt made haste to pay their debts, and every body was ready to lend cowry money to start all sorts of new enterprises. A company was organized, for example,

rates of interest, which can now be done to any extent required — but absolutely part with them for other kinds of property."—*Views of Enoch Ensley, of Memphis, Tennessee, on the National Finances*, Memphis, September, 1875.

with a capital of ten million cowries, to explore the wreck of the original ship which brought Robinson Crusoe to the island; and although nobody knew exactly where the wreck was, or what was supposed to remain in it, it was advocated as affording great opportunity for labor. Another project, for which a company with fifty million cowries capital was started, was to build a system of canals across the island, although the island had a width of only about ten miles, with a remarkably safe ocean navigation all around it.

Finally, the secret of the whole matter gradually leaked out. Other people besides the original three shrewd fellows found out where the supply of cowries came from, and made haste to visit the remote island, provide themselves with money, and put it in circulation. But the more money that was issued, the more was needed to supply the wants of trade, until at last it took a four-horse wagon-load of cowries to buy a bushel of wheat. Then the bubble burst. Stock-companies all failed. Trade became utterly stagnant. The man whom Robinson Crusoe had made secretary of the island treasury thought he could help matters by issuing a few more cowries, but it was no use. Some very wise persons were certain that every thing would be all right again if people would only have confidence; but as long as the people who worked and saved were uncertain what they were to receive for the products of their labor—something or nothing—confidence didn't return. Every body felt poor and swindled. Every body who thought he had money in savings-banks woke up all at once to the realization that his money was nothing but a lot of old shells. Every body had his bags, his tills, and his money-boxes filled with shells, which he had taken in exchange for commodities which had cost him valuable time and labor. Strictly speaking, however, calamity did not overtake every body.

There were some exceptions, namely the shrewd and idle fellows who had first found the cheap supply of cówries, and, taking advantage of the ignorance of the community, had added them to the before-existing circulation to serve as money. All these had taken very good care to keep the substantial valuable things—houses, lots, plows, grain, etc.—which they had received in exchange. They had, in fact, grown rich by robbing the rest of the community.* The community, however, were too courteous to call them thieves, and in conversation they were usually referred to as shrewd financiers, and as men ahead of their time. The concluding act of this curious island experience was, that the formerly so highly prized money became depreciated to such an extent as to possess value only as a material for making lime. The people accordingly, by burning, made lime out of it, and then, in order to make things outwardly cheerful, used the lime as whitewash. But upon one point they were all unanimous, and that was, that the next commodity they might select to use as money should be something whose permanency of value did not depend on elements capable of being suddenly affected by accidental circumstances, or arbitrarily and easily changed by

---

* "In the midst of the public distress, one class prospered greatly—the bankers; and, among the bankers, none could, in skill or in luck, bear a comparison with Charles Duncombe. He had been, not many years before, a goldsmith of very moderate wealth. He had probably, after the fashion of his craft, plied for customers under the arcades of the Royal Exchange, had saluted merchants with profound bows, and had begged to be allowed the honor of keeping their cash. But so dexterously did he now avail himself of the opportunities of profit which the general confusion of prices gave to a money-changer, that, at the moment when the trade of the kingdom was depressed to the lowest point, he laid down near ninety thousand pounds for the estate of Helmsley, in the North Riding of Yorkshire."—MACAULAY'S *History of England, State of the Currency in* 1694-'95.

the devices of those who desired to get their living without working for it.

But this experience of the islanders in reference to the originating and using of money, although curious, has not been exceptional; for the records of history show that men almost everywhere, in going through the process of civilization, have had a greater or less measure of the same experience. One particularly noteworthy illustration of this is recorded in the "History of New York," by Diedrich Knickerbocker, and in the manuscript records of the New York Historical Society. It was in the days of Dutch rule—1659—in New Amsterdam (afterward New York), when the common money in use was the so-called Indian money, or "wampum;" which consisted "of strings of beads wrought of clams, periwinkles, and other shell-fish. These had formed a simple currency among the savages, who were content to take them of the Dutch in exchange for peltries."

William Kieft was at that time governor, and being desirous of increasing the wealth of New Amsterdam, and withal, as the historian relates, somewhat emulous of Solomon (who made gold and silver as plenty as stones in the streets of Jerusalem), he (the governor) determined to accomplish his desire, and at the same time rival Solomon by making this money of easy production the current coin of the province. "It is true, it had an intrinsic value among the Indians, who used it to ornament their robes and moccasins; but among the honest burghers it had no more intrinsic value" than bits of bone, rag, paper, or any other worthless material. "This consideration, however, had no weight with Governor Kieft. He began by paying all the servants of the company, and all the debts of the Government, in strings of wampum. He sent emissaries to sweep the shores of Long Island, which was the Ophir of this modern Solomon, and abounded in shell-fish. These were transported in loads to New Amsterdam, coined into Indian money, and launched into circulation."

"And now for a time affairs went on swimmingly. Money became as plentiful as in the modern days of paper currency, and, to use a popular phrase, 'a wonderful impulse was given to public prosperity.'"

Unfortunately for the success of Governor Kieft's scheme, the Yankees on Connecticut River soon found that they could make wampum in any quantity, with little labor and cost, out of oyster-shells, and accordingly made haste to supply all the wampum that the wants of trade in New Amsterdam required; buying with it every thing that was offered, and paying the worthy Dutchmen their own price. Governor Kieft's money, it is to be further noticed, had also in perfection that most essential attribute of all good money, "*non-exportability*." Accordingly, when the Dutchmen wanted any tin pans or wooden bowls of Yankee manufacture, they had to pay for them in substantial guilders, or other sound metallic currency; wampum being no more acceptable to the Yankees in exchange than addled eggs, rancid butter, rusty pork, rotten potatoes, or any other non-exportable Dutch commodity.*

The result of all this was, that in a little time the Dutch-

---

* "Beyond the sea, in foreign lands, it (the greenback) fortunately is not money; but, sir, when have we had such a long and unbroken career of prosperity in business as since we adopted this non-exportable currency?"—*Speech of Hon. William D. Kelley, House of Representatives*, 1870.

"I desire the dollar to be made of such material, for the purpose, that it shall never be exported or desirable to carry out of the country. Framing an American system of finance, I do not propose to adapt it to the wants of any other nation."—*Speech of General B. F. Butler before the New York Board of Trade*, October 14th, 1875.

men and the Indians got all the wampum, and the Yankees all the beaver-skins, Dutch herrings, Dutch cheeses, and all the silver and gold of the province. Then, as might naturally have been expected, confidence became impaired. Trade also came to a stand-still, and, to quote from the old manuscript records, "the company is defrauded of her revenues, and the merchants disappointed in making returns with which they might wish to meet their engagements." It is safe to conclude that, after this, the commodity made use of by the Dutchmen as money was something less liable to have its value impaired than wampum.

The early settlers in East Tennessee also came to a similar conclusion, after a somewhat similar experience. Raccoon-skins were in demand for various purposes, and consequently were valuable. They accordingly selected them for use as money. Opossum-skins, on the other hand, were not in demand, and therefore had little value. Those of the settlers who desired to discharge their obligations without giving a full equivalent paid their taxes in opossum-skins to which coons' tails were attached. The counterfeits having once got into the treasury, could not be exported out of the treasury to meet the payments of the State, and the use of coon-skins as currency came to an end.

But to return to the island. Although the first experience of the islanders in selecting a commodity to be used as money had been particularly unfortunate, the necessity of having some agency to serve the purpose of money remained as great as before, and consequently a new commodity had to be selected. Various people proposed various things. Some proposed to use bananas, which were always desirable, and, when good and ripe, were always exchangeable at a very constant value; but their unfitness to be used as money was acknowledged as soon as it was pointed out that bananas decayed very quickly after they became most useful, and that therefore a man who had plenty of money to-day might have none to-morrow, and that through no fault of his own.* Wheat, cattle, and pieces of stamped iron were also proposed, but all of these were found to be unsuitable in some essential particular. Thus, for example, it was objected to wheat, that, though it was almost always in demand, and represented a very constant amount of labor for its production, it was too bulky to carry about, and rarely had the same exact value one year as another; to cattle, that it was impossible to divide up an ox, cutting off the tail at one time and the ears at another, for the purpose of making change, without destroying the value of the animal as a whole; and that if cows in general were to be used as legal tender to pay debts, the very poorest cow would very probably be selected from the money-pen for such a purpose;† while, if iron were adopted as money, and circu-

---

* "Some years since, Mademoiselle Zélie, a singer of the Théâtre Lyrique at Paris, made a professional tour round the world, and gave a concert in the Society Islands. In exchange for an air from 'Norma,' and a few other songs, she was to receive a third part of the receipts. When counted, her share was found to consist of three pigs, twenty-three turkeys, forty-four chickens, five thousand cocoa-nuts, besides considerable quantities of bananas, lemons, and oranges. At the Halle (market) in Paris, the prima donna remarks, in her lively letter printed by M. Walowski, this amount of live stock and vegetables might have brought four thousand francs, which would have been good remuneration for five songs. In the Society Islands, however, pieces of money were very scarce; and as mademoiselle could not consume any considerable portion of the receipts herself, it became necessary in the mean time to feed the pigs and poultry with the fruit."—JEVONS's *Money and Mechanism of Exchange.*

† In 1658, it was ordered by the General Court of Massachusetts that no man should pay taxes "in lank cattle."—FELT's *Massachusetts Currency.*

lated at its current value, it might be necessary to move about a ton to pay a debt of twenty or thirty dollars.

A peculiar kind of beads, made of blue glass, had come into use with the women on the island as ornaments, and being greatly in demand, small in bulk, and of most durable material, they were thought to be peculiarly well fitted to serve the purpose of money. They were accordingly adopted, and for a time fairly answered the purpose. But all at once the women declared their continued use to be unfashionable; and all use and demand for the beads at once ceasing, the merchants and others who had accumulated a large stock of them, in exchange for other commodities, at the same moment found that what they had regarded as money had no longer any purchasing power or value, and in consequence experienced great losses. Thereupon the community concluded not to use blue glass beads any longer as money.*

How fast the people on the island, by reason of their varied experience, educated themselves up to a knowledge of what constitutes good money may be inferred from the following incident:

A portion of the inhabitants on the island were heathen, and, to defray the expense of efforts to civilize and Christianize them, it was the habit of certain good men to take advantage of the assembling of the people from time to time to solicit and receive contributions for such objects. It was observed, however, on such occasions that some persons, either through ignorance of what constitutes money, or by reason of great poverty, were in the habit of depositing commodities in the hat which were not money; and the practice having

* This incident is related by Burton, in his " Explorations of the Lake Regions of Central Africa" (1858–'59), as one within his knowledge of actual occurrence.

been brought to the attention of Robinson Crusoe (who generally presided at such meetings), he is reported to have administered rebuke and instruction in the following impressive manner:

"Before proceeding to take up our regular contribution for the heathen," he said, " I would suggest to the congregation—and more especially to those who sit in the gallery—that the practice of putting into the hat commodities which are not money, more especially buttons, shows a degree of ignorance respecting the uses of money on the part of some in this community which I had not supposed possible, after all our recent and varied experience on this subject. But if, through ignorance or impecuniosity, any should feel obliged to continue to contribute buttons in the place of money, I would request that they do not stamp down or break off the eyes; inasmuch, as while by so doing they utterly destroy the utility of these commodities as buttons, and do not increase their desirability as money, they also utterly fail to deceive the heathen; who, although ignorant of the Gospel, and not using buttons for any purpose, are nevertheless, as a general thing, good judges of currency."

CHAPTER VI.

GOLD, AND HOW THEY CAME TO USE IT.

FINALLY, time and circumstances helped the islanders to a solution of their difficulties. A man, walking in a ravine one day, picked up a small bright mass of shining metal. Although it had evidently lain in the sand, been washed by the water, exposed to the atmosphere, and rubbed against the rocks, nobody knows how long, it had a remarkable brightness and color; and the more it was rubbed, the brighter and more attractive it became. This little mass of metal, which afterward came to be designated as gold, the man carried home to his wife, who in turn was so much pleased with it that she hung it by a string about her neck as an ornament. Its attractiveness of course excited the desire of every other woman to have the same, and a further search in the ravine resulted in the discovery of other nuggets. Closer examination of the new metal also showed that it possessed many other remarkable qualities besides brightness. It was found it could easily be melted and cast, and also be readily molded without heat by hammering and pressing; and that when so cast, molded, and pressed, it persistently retained the shape and impression that were given it. Further, that it could be drawn into the finest of wire, hammered into the thinnest of plates and leaves, and be bent and twisted to almost any extent without breaking; that an admixture with it of the slightest impurity or alloy so immediately changed its color, that color became to a very high degree a test of its purity;* that fire, water, air, and almost all the agencies destructive to other things, had comparatively little or no effect upon it; that with the exception of size and weight, every piece, no matter how small, possessed all the attributes of every other larger piece; and that when any large piece was divided into a great number of smaller pieces, these last, in turn, could be reunited without loss or difficulty again into one whole. Of course, the discovery of all these remarkable qualities united in one substance not only greatly increased its utility, but at the same time greatly increased the desire of every body to have it. In place of being worn in a rough state as an ornament, it was converted into rings, bracelets, chains, pins, etc. It was found to be almost indispensable for a great number of mechanical and chemical purposes; and, finally, the charm for its possession and desire for its use proved so overpower-

---

* In one of the mints there is exhibited as a curiosity a case in which this fact is demonstrated in the most striking manner. It contains some fifty or more very thin ribbons, or strips, of gold, half an inch wide by three inches in length, placed in a row, parallel to, but separated from each other by a slight interval. The first ribbon is composed of gold of the highest standard of purity; the second differs from the first to the extent of one per cent. of admixture with a baser metal; while the third contains two per cent., the fourth three per cent., and so on, until in the last ribbon, or strip, the amount of gold and alloy is equal. The color of the first ribbon is, in the highest sense of the term, golden or typical. The color of the second differs from the first by a shade, which shade in every successive ribbon changes and becomes more and more marked as the proportion of alloy entering into its composition increases: and so peculiar are these differences of color that it is possible for an individual unskilled in metallurgy, but having access to the standard, to make a comparatively accurate test of the purity of any article of gold in his possession by a simple comparison of color.

ing that to many it actually became almost an object of worship.

If a man was a Pagan, he felt that in no way could he so honor and symbolize the god he worshiped as to fashion in gold the image of that which he imagined; if he was a Christian, he chose gold for the fabrication of his symbolic vessels and ornaments, as, of all material things, the one which was most typical of purity, beauty, durability, and worth. If a great government or a people desired to commemorate the deeds of a hero or statesman, it impressed their effigies in medals of gold; if a maxim was enunciated which by general consent embodied the best rules of life, it was called golden; if a law or precept was thought worthy of being kept in ever-present remembrance before the people, it was emblazoned in letters of gold; while for speech, prophecy, or poetry, this same metal has ever been a never-failing source for the finest of comparisons and the most attractive of figurative illustrations. In short, from the time of its first discovery, among all nations, in all countries, with the ignorant and the learned, the savage and the civilized, the rich and the poor, the humble and the powerful, gold has always been, of all material things, the one which most men have desired most; the one for which, under most circumstances, they have been willing to exchange all other material possessions, and for the sake of acquiring which, even part with immaterial things of greater value—honor, creed, morality, health, and even life itself.

Gold so becoming an object of universal desire to the people on the island, and made exchangeable for all other things, it soon acquired spontaneously a universal purchasing power, and from that moment became *Money.*

This purchasing power was at first by no means fixed or constant. So long as there was but a small quantity of gold, its purchasing power was large. As the quantity extracted from the rocks or washed from the sands became greater, and the wants of the people became more and more satisfied, its purchasing power or value decreased; and if the supply had continued, and the demand had been limited to the wants of the island exclusively, its value in time would have undoubtedly been no greater than copper or iron, and possibly not so great. But, very curiously, an abundant supply did not continue. That which was obtained first and with little labor proved to be the result of the decay and washing of the rocks through long ages; and when the readily accessible or surface deposits became exhausted, as was soon the case, the conditions determining the supply of gold became altogether different. On the one hand, there was no lack of gold. Instead of being a very scarce metal, as was for a time supposed, it was found to be so widely disseminated that the chemists and metallurgists readily detected traces of gold in almost every extensive bed of clay and sand they examined.*

---

* In 1862 Mr. Eckfelt, then principal assayer at the mint in Philadelphia, communicated to the American Philosophical Society the result of some exceedingly curious examinations demonstrating the very wide distribution of gold. The city of Philadelphia, he stated, was underlaid by a bed of clay having an area of about ten square miles, with an average depth of about fifteen feet. Specimens of this clay—all natural deposits—taken from such localities as might furnish a fair assay of the whole—the cellar of the market on Market Street, near Eleventh, and from a brick-yard in the suburbs of the city—all yielded, on careful analysis, small amounts of gold; the average amount indicated being seven-tenths of a grain—or about three cents' worth—of gold for every cubit foot of clay. Assuming these data to be correct, the value of the gold, according to Mr. Eckfelt, which lies securely buried underneath the streets and houses of Philadelphia must therefore be equivalent to $128,000,000; or if we include all the clay contained in the corporate limits, the amount of gold contained

But, on the other hand, experience also proved that to collect any very considerable quantity of the metal required the expenditure not only of a vast amount of most disagreeable and exhausting labor, but also of a great quantity of other commodities. So that the people who, at the outset, abandoned their various occupations of raising wheat, making coats, building boats, baking bread, and constructing stone walls and chimneys, and betook themselves to digging gold, soon learned that, as a general rule, the results of a day's labor thus employed purchased no more of useful or desirable commodities— meat, drink, clothes, etc.—than the results of a similar amount of labor exerted in the most ordinary occupations; and not a few even were ready to assert, as the result of their individual experience, that a man could do better for himself in the way of earning a living by following any and every other occupation rather than that of seeking for gold.* Accordingly, after trying it for a little while, the most skilled laborers left the gold regions and went back to their old occupations; and these, in turn, were followed by the unskilled laborers in such

---

in it must be equal to all that has yet been obtained from California and Australia.

"It is also apparent," says Mr. Eckfelt, "that every time a cart-load of clay is hauled out of a cellar in Philadelphia, enough gold goes with it to pay for the carting; and if the bricks which front our houses could have brought to their surface, in the form of gold-leaf, the amount of gold which they contain, we should have the glittering show of two square inches on every brick."

* On the Rhine, near Strasburg, a good able-bodied laborer can earn on an average one franc seventy-five centimes per day, washing gold from the sands of the river; but, as under most circumstances he can earn ten sous more by working in the fields on the banks of the river, and without so much risk of getting rheumatism, gold-washing on the Rhine is not often adopted as a regular employment.

numbers, that had it not been for the encouragement growing out of the hope of suddenly enriching themselves through the chance discovery of a great nugget (as sometimes happened), the mines would have been entirely deserted. As it was, the supply of gold greatly fell off, and, the demand for it remaining about the same, the purchasing power of the stock on hand for other commodities gradually increased, until it came about that the result of an average day's labor in digging gold was found to buy *more* than the result of an average day's labor in other occupations. But as soon as this was observed, an additional supply of labor went back to gold-mining, and continued to follow it, until an equalization of results from effort in gold-digging and effort in other corresponding employments was again established, as before related. And this interchange of employments and equalization of results from labor went on, year by year, until at last the people, as it were by instinct, found out that a given quantity of gold represented more permanently a given amount of a certain grade or kind of human labor or effort than any other one substance. And the moment this fact became apparent, the people on the island for the first time also clearly perceived that gold, in addition to the universal exchanging quality or purchasing power which it had before naturally acquired, from the circumstance that every body from the time of its first discovery wanted it, had further acquired two other attributes, which fitted it, above all things else, to serve as money; namely, and *first*, that it had become a measure or standard of value, by which, as by a yard-stick, the comparative value of all other commodities might be measured or estimated; and, *second*, that its value or purchasing power was so constant and continuously inherent in itself, even under circumstances when the value of most other commodities would be destroyed, that the greatest security or guarantee which any person owning gold could possibly have of its remaining valuable to him for any length of time was, that the owner should simply keep possession of it.

By no portion of people on the island was this last attribute regarded so much in the light of a blessing as by the poor old men and women. As a general rule, they earned but little more than sufficed to support them, and they were therefore always naturally very anxious lest what little they saved should be impaired in value or made worthless by keeping, before the time when they might especially need it to pay for doctors and medicine, or insure them a decent burial. The cowry money, which had before represented their hard toil and personal deprivation, had turned out, on keeping, to be only worthless shells; the bead money had become valueless when it became unfashionable; the cattle money had to be fed every day to keep it from experiencing a heavy discount, and penned up every night to prevent it from walking off; the wheat money was always liable to be injured by damp or devoured by vermin; while twenty pounds of pig-iron had proved too heavy for their old limbs to carry to the store every time they wanted to purchase a little cloth or tobacco. But here was something at last which completely satisfied the necessities of their situation, and enabled them to feel certain that, whether they buried it in the ground, where it was always damp and moldy; or put it in the chimney, where it was always hot and smoky; or lived at one end of the island among the heathen, or at the other end among the Christians, would always, year in and year out, buy about the same average quantity of all sorts of things; and which, when offered in payment for services or commodities, to the doctor, lawyer, merchant, druggist, undertaker, mason, or tailor; to the Yankee, Irish, Dutch,

Turk, or Hindoo; to the governor of Ohio, or a senator from Indiana, did not require any of them to look in a book, examine a law, read the Bible, or hunt up the resolutions of the last Congress or political convention, to tell how much it was worth, or whether it was safe to take and keep it.

There was a very wise man on the island who objected to the use of gold as money, for the reason that he felt afraid that the poor old women who wanted to feel certain of having always something of reliable value in their possession would fill their old stockings with it and hoard it.* But he was soon shut up by some one asking him, why, if the old women wanted to keep something by them perfectly secure against a rainy day, and slept better nights because they knew they had it, they shouldn't be allowed that privilege? and if there could be any possible reason why any one should object to the old women hoarding gold, except that he wanted to cheat and wrong the poor by compelling them to keep their hard-earned savings in something whose value was not certain, and which might have no value whatever when it came time to pay the doctor or the undertaker?

When the people on the island first began to use gold as money, they carried it around with them in the form in which it was first found; the fine dust or scales inclosed in quills, and the nuggets in bags; or they melted and hammered it into

---

* "And when the substitution is made" (of a silver for a paper fractional currency), "what will be the consequence? The metal currency will have to be considerably debased, or else every old woman in the country will fill her stockings with it and bury it. It will be hoarded, sir; hoarded to the extent of removing millions from the currency of the country." The general paused, glared at a village wrapped in rain, by which we were rattling, chewed his cigar vigorously, and lapsed into silence.—*A Newspaper Reporter's Interview with General Butler*, September, 1875.

large lumps and bars;* and, as the purchasing power of the gold was always proportioned to its weight and purity, every body carried round with him small scales and tests with which he proved the gold before making exchanges with it (the same as is customary at the present day in China). But this method involved great inconveniences; and although the statement of a person of recognized honesty that he had proved the value of the gold he offered in payment was generally accepted, it was nevertheless recognized that there was no more unfairness or discourtesy in the claim of the grocer to test the quality of the money of his customer by scales and acids, than there was in the claim of the customer to test, by tasting, the salt and sugar of the grocer. As might be inferred, therefore, it often required a good deal of time to complete the most ordinary exchanges, and people everywhere complained about it and wrote letters to the newspapers. Merchants who were very cautious and particular, irritated their customers, and got the reputation of being very exacting and distrustful; while merchants who had but little capital and wanted to get business, advertised they would take gold on the simple word of their customers. But it was observed of the last, that, owing to being constantly cheated, they all, sooner or later, failed. At last the difficulty was remedied by a series of happy circumstances.

Robinson Crusoe had, some years before this, died, at a good old age, as had also Will Atkins, and all the sailors who had come with him to the island from other countries; so that there were none now on the island who had ever known any thing about or ever seen any coined money. In making some

---

* Gold in its crude state, and uncoined, was until recently in use as money in some parts of California, Mexico, and on the West Coast of Africa.

public improvements, however, a party of workmen one day broke into the old cave in which Crusoe had first lived when he escaped from the shipwreck, and there, in the dirt beneath the floor, were discovered the three great bags of money which Crusoe had found in the chest, and in his disgust had buried and utterly forgotten. Every body at once recognized the metal to be gold, and was perfectly willing to exchange other commodities for it with the finders, the same as he was willing to do for any other gold. But why it should be in the form of flat round disks, and stamped with inscriptions and images, was something that puzzled every body; and the Antiquarian and Philosophical Society called a special meeting to discuss the subject. Some, looking to only one side of the pieces, thought they were medals struck to commemorate some distinguished man, or a woman, whose name often appeared to be " Liberty." Others, who looked only at the other side, thought they were intended to signalize a great contest between the lion and the unicorn, or to make the people familiar with the peculiarities of some unnatural bird or beast, which, as it was not like any thing either in the heavens, or on the earth, or in the waters under the earth, it might not be sinful to worship.

At last, after the flat disks or coins had been for some time in circulation, and the community had found out, by repeatedly weighing and testing them, that each disk represented a constant weight of gold of uniform purity, the idea came at once to every one that the only use of the fanciful images and inscriptions on the disks was to officially testify to the fact of their uniformity of weight and value; and then every body wondered that he could have been so stupid as not to have before recognized the idea and adopted it, in place of every man weighing, cutting up, and testing his gold every time he desired to part with or receive it in making an exchange. An arrangement was accordingly at once made for a public establishment—afterward called a mint—to which every person who so desired could bring his gold and receive it back again after it had been divided into suitable pieces of determinate weight and fineness; the fact that the weight and fineness of each piece had been so proved being indicated by appropriate marks upon the metal. And in this manner "coined money" first came into use on the island. And by this time, also, the money which Robinson Crusoe found in the chest, and which, when it first came into his possession, had neither *utility, value,* nor use as a *standard,* or *measure of value,* had gradually acquired all these several attributes: *utility,* when the material of which it was composed became capable of satisfying some human desire for it, as an ornament, as a symbol of worship, or for some mechanical or chemical purpose; *value* (the sole result of labor), when it became an object *of* or equivalent *in* exchange, or acquired a power of purchasing other things; a *standard,* or *measure of value,* when its purchasing power, by reason of various circumstances, was found to be, if not absolutely permanent, at least more permanent, on the average, than that of any other commodity.

The conversion of money into coin was something purely artificial, and the result of law, or statute enactments, the sole object of which was simply to make the money (previously in use) true and in the highest degree convenient. But, as has already been pointed out, money came into use in the first instance without statute, and was the result, as it were, of men's instincts; and the subsequent choice by them of gold, in preference to any other commodities for use as money, was for reasons similar to those which induced men to choose silk, wool, flax, and cotton as materials for clothing; and stone, brick, and timber as materials for houses. It was the thing best adapted to supply the want needed.

The introduction and use of coined money at once gave an impetus to business, and made the people richer, because it saved time and labor in making exchanges, and relieved every man from the trouble and expense of buying and carrying round with him scales and other tests. The only persons dissatisfied were the scale-makers, who found their business almost destroyed, and they petitioned the authorities to have their interests protected by the enactment of a law compelling all persons to weigh their coins with scales before exchanging, as formerly they did their gold. But, as every body at once saw that the effect of such a law would be equivalent to compelling all exchangers to do useless work, the petition amounted to nothing.

For convenience in speaking and writing, also, each piece of gold or coin of determinate weight and fineness regularly issued by the mint received a particular name and had a particular device impressed on it. Thus, for example, the piece of lowest denomination, containing 25.8 grains of standard gold, which had on it a likeness of Crusoe's old and faithful servant, was called a " Friday;" a piece of ten times its weight and value, with a small portrait of the founder of the island community, was called a " Crusoe;" and a piece of double the weight of the last, or twenty times the weight of the first, with a large portrait on it, was called a " Robinson Crusoe " or a " double Crusoe." Some time after, when the island became generally known to the rest of the world, it was found that these coins exactly corresponded in weight, fineness, and value with those adopted in that foreign country called the United States, and there known under the names of the gold dollar, eagle, and double-eagle; and after a time, for the purpose of favoring the development of civilization and assimilating nationalities by the adoption of a common monetary standard, it was agreed to discard all local sentiments, and to substitute the latter names for the former.

CHAPTER VII.

HOW THE ISLANDERS DETERMINED TO BE AN HONEST AND FREE PEOPLE.

NEXT came the consideration of the laws regulating the exchanges and the use of money. Some people wanted laws enacted that every person should be obliged to sell and part with any thing he owned, provided a nominal or real equivalent in what the State should declare money should be offered him; and, also, that when any person had bought commodities and services of another, and had promised to pay for them after a time, he might fully discharge the obligation by tendering that which the State said was money, no matter whether in the mean time the persons in charge of the mint had, for any reasons, taken out one-half the valuable gold in the coins, and substituted in its place comparatively worthless lead.

But, to the honor of the islanders, these propositions met with little favor. They said, we mean to be an honest and also a free people; and, therefore, every one in buying or selling shall do exactly what he has agreed to do; unless, by reason of some unforeseen or unavoidable circumstances, he is absolutely unable to perform his agreement or contract. And they said, further, that if any one receives commodities and services, and promises to give, five years or five minutes afterward, in re-

THE SURVIVAL OF THE FITTEST.

turn, an agreed-upon quality and quantity of gold, wheat, cod-fish, or cabbages, it shall be considered, as in truth it is, dishonest to attempt to discharge the obligation by offering pig-iron in the place of gold, pease or beans in the place of wheat, soft-shell crabs in the place of cod-fish, or pumpkins in the place of cabbages; and any community which shall in any way sanction any such evasion of the letter or spirit of its obligations can have no rightful claim to call itself an honest, Christian people; and if any community enacts and maintains laws *compelling* any person to receive in exchange, or in pay for his services or products, something which he did not agree to and would not otherwise receive, such a community has no rightful claim to call itself a free community. The people on the island, therefore, decided that they would allow the island authorities to interfere with exchanges to this extent only: that the medium of exchange and measure of values that they had adopted and called a Friday, or a dollar, should always and under all circumstances contain 25.8 grains of standard gold; that this standard should never be departed from; and that although no one should be compelled to use it, yet whenever any one talked about or promised to pay or give money, without specifying whether the money should be wampum money, bead money, cattle money, gold money, or any other particular kind of money, the money issued by the acknowledged authorities of the island should be understood and accepted as what was meant. In short, like sensible men, the islanders concluded that as long as they maintained in common use a real, good, and true money, which carried on its face evidence (easily read and known of all men) of its value or purchasing power, there was little use of cumbering up the statute-book with any thing about legal tender. They would leave that to other people wiser than they were, who desired

to use money that would not circulate, except it had some artificial power or agency back of it to make it go.

After this, every thing for a time pertaining to trade and
commerce went on very smoothly on the island. It is true
there were bad persons who obtained commodities and services on credit for which they never intended to pay; careless
and extravagant persons who bought more than they were
able to pay for; and foolish and oversanguine people who,
after having by labor and economy accumulated a good store
of commodities, exchanged them for shares in enterprises
which never could pay.   And when people by one or more of
such methods lost the results of their hard labor and toil, they
naturally felt depressed, lost confidence in their fellow-men,
and thought times and things might be improved by turning
all those in office out, and putting new men in.   But no one
on the island ever for a moment imagined that there was any
way to honestly replace the money they had lost, except by
acquiring through industry and economy a new store of useful commodities with which to buy money; and no one who
ever had any thing to sell which others in the community
wanted, and were able to give in return a fair equivalent, ever
found himself in want of money or a market; while, on the
other hand, no one who had nothing to sell which the community wanted or were able to pay for ever succeeded in obtaining either money or a market.

CHAPTER VIII.

HOW THE PEOPLE ON THE ISLAND CAME TO USE CURRENCY IN THE PLACE OF MONEY.

As time went on, changes in the method of doing business gradually occurred on the island. Instead of being an isolated and unknown community, their existence as an organized, civilized state became generally known to the rest of the world, and a brisk trade and commerce resulted from the exchange of the products of the island for the products of other countries. An excellent harbor existed at each end of the island, and about these points the population naturally aggregated, and built up two very considerable towns. The middle of the island, on the other hand, was elevated into high mountain ranges, covered with dense forests, in crossing which travelers journeying between the two cities were often robbed of all the gold they carried about them. To obviate this danger, and avoid the necessity of carrying gold, persons living at opposite ends of the island, therefore, adopted a system of giving written orders for money on each other, which each reciprocally agreed to pay to the person whose name was written in the order or draft, and then periodically settled or balanced their accounts by offsetting one order or payment against another. In this way value or purchasing power was transmitted long distances much more cheaply and conveniently than could be effected by the transmission of gold itself; and also much more safely, inasmuch as the thieves could make no use of the orders, even if they obtained them. And thus it was that the people on the island became acquainted with and first used what were afterward known as "*bills of exchange.*"*

This labor-saving and danger-avoiding device, moreover, proved so useful, that the idea soon suggested itself that by an extension of the principle involved in the bill of exchange the necessity of carrying gold at all in any quantity might also be avoided. A public office was therefore established, where people might deposit their gold under the guardianship of the state, and receive a ticket or receipt for the amount, payable in coin on demand; which tickets, from the fact that every body knew that they were convertible into gold at will, and that no more tickets were issued than corresponded to gold actually deposited and retained, soon came to be regarded as equally good and valid as gold itself, and vastly more convenient for the purpose of making exchanges. And thus it was that *currency* (from the Latin *curro*, to run) originated and came into use on the island as a substitute and representative of money.† The

---

* Historically, bills of exchange probably originated with the Jews of the Middle Ages, who, ever liable to persecution, adopted a system of drafts, or written orders, upon one another, which each agreed to honor and pay to the person named in the draft.

† It was in this manner that the first bank of which we have any record originated in 1171, namely, the Bank of the Republic of Venice. Venice in that year was at war and needed money. The Council of Ten, or the Government, called upon the merchants to bring in their gold or coin into the public treasury, and gave credit on the books of the state for the amounts so deposited; which credits carried interest (always promptly paid) at the rate of four per cent. per annum. Soon after the establishment of this bank one of the depositors died; and it becoming necessary to distribute his estate among five children, his bank-credit was divided into five portions and transferred to five new owners. A system of transferring bank-credits was thus introduced, and proved so useful that in a brief time the merchants adopted it very generally as a means of paying

name originally given to these receipts was first " bank-cred-its," and then " bank-notes," but after a time people acquired a habit of designating them as " paper money." But this latter term was conceded to be but a mere fiction of speech and a bad use of language ; for every intelligent person at once saw that a promise to deliver a commodity, or an acknowledg-ment of the receipt of, or a title to, a thing, could not possibly be the commodity or the thing itself, any more than a shadow could be the substance, or the picture of a horse a horse, or the smell of a good dinner the same as the dinner itself.

Nevertheless, as an instrumentality for transferring com-modities used for money, and avoiding the loss and waste un-avoidable in handling and transporting such commodities, the currency thus devised was a great invention, and being always represented by, or, as we may express it, covered with, the com-modity—gold—which, of all things, fluctuates least in value, it perfectly answered the purpose of money, without actually be-ing so. It also furnished another striking illustration of the superiority of the commodity gold to serve either as money or as an object of value for deposit, against which receipts or certificates of deposit might be issued to serve as currency ; for if other valuable commodities, like cattle, corn, cloth, or coal, had been selected for a like purpose, the bank would have been obliged to erect large pens, sheds, and warehouses for the storing of the deposits ; and, let them be guarded ever so carefully, their value or purchasing power would, after a time, rapidly diminish from natural and unavoidable causes.

---

balances in all great business transactions. The banks of Amsterdam and of Hamburg were also subsequently established on substantially the same basis, and are doing business to-day successfully. The Bank of Venice did business for five hundred years ; during which period the state was prosperous, and there were few failures among the mercantile classes.

A SHADOW IS NOT A SUBSTANCE.

The value of most commodities, even in a perfect condition, furthermore differs so much by reasons of mere locality, that there could be no possible uniformity in the value of the receipt for the deposit of one and the same article, issued by banks in different places, to serve as currency; the value or purchasing power of a ton of coal, or a fat ox, being one thing at the mouth of a coal-mine or on a prairie stock-farm, and quite a different thing ten, twenty, or a hundred miles distant. But in the case of gold, the space needed to store up what represents a vast value is very small, while the value or purchasing power of gold not only is, but is certain to remain, on the average, very constant all the world over.*

---

* If to any it may seem puerile and unnecessary to enter into such explanations, it may be well to remind them that one of the schemes for a new currency, which has of late found some earnest advocates in the United States, is that of Josiah Warren, of Ohio, who proposed that currency "should be issued by those men, women, and children who perform useful service"—*i. e.*, grow corn, mine coal, catch cod-fish, pick up chestnuts and the like—"but by nobody else;" such results of service being deposited in safe receptacles, and having receipts of deposit issued against them to serve as "equitable money." A further axiom of Mr. Warren was, "that the most disagreeable labor" (not the most useful) "is entitled to the highest compensation;" and, therefore, inferentially entitled to issue the most money. A specimen of this equitable money before the writer reads as follows:

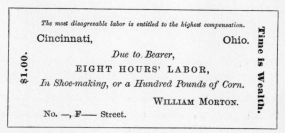

The most disagreeable labor is entitled to the highest compensation.

Cincinnati,   Ohio.

$1.00.   *Due to Bearer*,

EIGHT HOURS' LABOR,

In Shoe-making, or a Hundred Pounds of Corn.

WILLIAM MORTON.

No. —, F—— Street.

Time is Wealth.

Of course, to make this money equitable, and its issue, as claimed, "the satisfactory solution of the great problem of labor and capital," there must be some presupposed equitable relation between eight hours of shoe-making and a hundred pounds of corn. But one hundred pounds of corn in Illinois are the result of only a quarter as much labor as a hundred pounds in New England; and what comparison is there between eight hours' work of a skilled mechanic and that of a mere cobbler in making shoes? or of the man who performs a disagreeable, slavish piece of work, and of the

CHAPTER IX.

WAR WITH THE CANNIBALS, AND WHAT CAME OF IT.

But more serious matters than the making and issuing of money soon claimed the attention of the people of the island. It will be remembered that Friday was first brought to the

genius who invents or makes a machine that makes this disagreeable work unnecessary?

E. D. Linton, of Boston, one of Warren's most eminent disciples, improves on Warren's ideas, and proposes that the United States Government should prepare and issue a currency, which should read as follows:

> *The United States will pay One Dollar to Bearer, on demand, in —— bushels of Illinois Fall Wheat, at United States No. 1 Store-house, No. 12 River Street, Chicago, Ill.*
>
> ——
>
> This note is receivable for all debts due the United States.

And the same inferentially in respect to pigs, coal, shoes, and the services of doctors, lawyers, and cooks. So, then, if the note is not to be on its face a lie, and the promise is to be actually performed on demand, the necessity will be absolute on the part of the Government of the United States to have store-houses for wheat at Chicago, pig-pens at Peoria, coal-mines or dépôts at Pottsville, and trained professionals ready on call to plead a case, preach a sermon, cure a cold, and cook a dinner; and all of these last must take their pay in pigs if required. But as a pig has one value at Peoria, and another value at almost every other place, the dollar's worth of pig which the United States would pay might be a whole pig in one place, a half in another, and possibly only the snout in another.

WAR WITH THE CANNIBALS, AND WHAT CAME OF IT. 61

island by the cannibals, for the purpose of being cooked and eaten, and that he was rescued from this fate by the valor of Robinson Crusoe, as was subsequently also Friday's father and others of his countrymen. But the cannibals, although then repulsed, did not at the same time lose their appetites, or the remembrance of the good cheer that had escaped them; and meat becoming scarce in their own country, they projected a grand invasion of the island, with the intent of capturing and cooking Friday, if he was still there, or, in default of Friday, any body and every body they might happen to catch. The islanders all at once, therefore, found themselves precipitated into a terrible war, and were obliged to struggle not only for their homes, but for their individual existence.

The Government was active and energetic, but to carry on the war a vast expenditure of commodities was necessary; and as the Government of the island—in common with all other governments—never had, or could have, any commodities or money to buy commodities with, other than what it obtained through loans and taxes, the people, one and all, were called upon to help. There was, however, some fear that if the calls for help were put in the form of taxes, the fires of patriotism might not burn as brightly as was desirable, and it was therefore deemed expedient to say little about taxes at the outset, and rely mainly on loans, to be repaid after the war was over.

The people, on their side, responded most cheerfully. Some gave one thing and some another. Some gave service as soldiers, laborers, and artificers; others contributed timber for canoes, cloth for tents, iron for spear-heads and guns, corn and flour, hay, medicines, and money—in short, all sorts of useful things, the results of previous labor and economy on the part of the individual contributors. In return, the contributors received back from the Government a promise, expressed on paper, to repay the commodities borrowed, or their value in money. These promises were of two kinds. In one the promise was made definite as to the time of its fulfillment, and the amount or value of the promise carried interest. These were called *bonds*. In the other, the promise, although definite, specified no particular time for making it good, and its amount or value was not subject to interest. These latter, from the circumstance that they were written on blue paper, were popularly termed "bluebacks." When the people got the bonds, they put them carefully away, for the sake of the interest that would accumulate upon them; but when they got the bluebacks, they were at first at a loss to know what to do with them. They were in some respects unlike any thing they had ever seen before; and yet there was a very close resemblance between them and the certificates of deposits of gold in the public repository, which they had now been in the habit for some time of using as currency. And as the one promised, on the part of the Government, to pay money equally with the other, there seemed to the public to be no good reason why one should not be used as the representative and equivalent of money as readily as the other.

The real difference was, that their former currency, composed of tickets or certificates given in exchange for a deposit of actual gold, represented an actual accumulation of an equivalent of every thing desirable which labor could produce all the world over; while, on the other hand, the promises to pay which the island authorities issued in exchange for the commodities loaned them by the people, and subsequently used up in fighting the cannibals, represented an actual destruction of almost every thing useful and desirable in place of accumulation. The people, however, did not see this; and by reason of not seeing it they continued to accept and regard the promises to pay, which represented loss and destruction, as the same thing as money, and naturally also as wealth; and as the creation and issue of this sort of money or wealth increased as destruction increased, they finally, one and all, came to the conclusion that the more and faster they destroyed, the richer they should all be; and that, by a happy series of accidents, they had at last solved that great problem which the world had so long been anxious about—namely, "of how to eat your cake and at the same time keep it." And, as a further illustration of the extent to which this idea acquired a hold upon the public mind, it may be mentioned that some of the most popular books which were published about this time on the island had the following suggestive titles: "*A National Debt a National Blessing;*" "*Don't Pay as you Go, a sure Way to Get Rich;*" "*Pulling at your Boot-straps the best Way to Rise in the World,*" and the like.

Undoubtedly one great reason which encouraged the people of the island in their delusion was the circumstance that the Government promises to pay, although they had ceased to represent accumulation, or a definite equivalent of any thing in particular, did not thereby cease to be instrumentalities for effecting exchanges; but, on the contrary, continued to constitute great labor-saving machines, performing a work precisely similar in character to that performed by a ship or a locomotive—namely, the removal of obstacles between the producer and consumer. But, in becoming *a representative of a debt to be paid* in place of representing *a means of paying a debt*, the new currency lost at once the really most important quality of good money; inasmuch as it ceased to be a *common* equivalent, or *in itself an object of value* in exchange, and therefore became incapable of properly discharging the function of

a standard, or measure, for estimating the comparative value
of other things; resembling, in this deficiency, a ship without
a rudder, or a locomotive without a track to run on. The removal of a rudder from a ship, or the taking up the track in
front of a locomotive does not impair the capacity of the one
for cargo, or the power of the other for pulling. But if it is
attempted to use a ship or a locomotive under such circumstances for the purposes for which they were constructed—*i. e.*,
as agencies for effecting and facilitating exchanges—the result
of their work will be so uncertain and hazardous that the owners of the things to be exchanged would require large insurance
against the possible action of the exchanging agencies. And
so it was with this blueback currency of the island, which,
ceasing to represent or be convertible on demand into a constant quantity of any commodity, ceased to be a constant
equivalent or measure of value of any thing.

If the news came one day that the cannibals had been repulsed, a given number of the bluebacks would buy a bushel
of wheat. If the news came the next day that the black
troops, although they had fought nobly, had been driven back,
and that there was some prospect that every body, sooner or
later, would be cooked and eaten, then the same number of
bluebacks bought only half the quantity of wheat. Consequently, every body, in selling commodities representing expenditure of time and labor, added to the price of the same,
in order to insure himself against the fluctuations of the
purchasing power of the currency he received; or, in other
words, to make sure that what he received should remain,
for a greater or less length of time, the equivalent of what
he gave. But as no one could tell what the cannibals were
likely to do from day to day, and therefore what were to be

the fluctuations in the purchasing power of the currency, every body in selling any thing felt that he incurred a risk, in addition to the risks usually attendant upon ordinary buying and selling. And as the data for estimating these risks were just as uncertain as the data for estimating the results of dice-throwing, every body guessed at the amount of insurance needed, or, what is the same thing, *bet* on the purchasing power of the currency at future periods. An abnormal gambling character, therefore, necessarily became a part of every business transaction, and worked to the great detriment of all that class of people on the islands, who had only labor to sell, which loses its entire value for the time, if not bought at the moment it is offered for sale, and the selling price of which, when once established, can only be changed with difficulty. And as this was a very important matter in the financial history of the island, it is desirable to illustrate it by relating the details of what actually happened:

The people on the island clothed themselves largely in cloth made in foreign countries; and as the island currency was non-exportable, the cloth was paid for by exporting gold, or commodities which could readily be exchanged in other countries for gold. The cloth thus purchased with gold was made up into clothing by the "ready-made" clothing dealers in the cities, and sold in this form for currency, to smaller or retail dealers on a credit of from three to six or nine months. Had the currency involved in this transaction throughout been gold, or certificates representing deposits of gold, the credit price of the ready-made clothing would have been the *cash* price, with a small amount additional to represent interest on the credit-time, and a possible risk of non-payment; and the seller would never for one moment have taken into consideration the question whether the currency, or representation of money in which he was to be paid, three, six, or nine months afterward, would have the same value or purchasing power that it had on the day the debt was contracted. He might have doubted whether his customer would pay him at all, but he never would as to the quality of that which he was entitled to receive as payment. But as the currency involved in so much of the transaction as occurred after the cloth was made into clothing was neither gold nor any thing which represented gold, nor any other valuable commodity, and therefore, like a ship without a rudder, or a locomotive without a track, was sure to be unreliable as an exchanging instrumentality, the seller knew to a certainty that *what* he was to receive in payment of his goods, three, six, or nine months afterward, would not have the same value or purchasing power that it had on the day the debt was contracted. It might be greater, it might be less; but the seller never bet on the former contingency, or allowed for it by deducting any thing from the time price of his goods, for to do so would be to discard in anticipation a possible incidental profit. But he always, as a matter of safety, felt obliged to *bet* on the latter contingency, and then cover the bet by adding correspondingly to the price of every thing he sold on credit. When, by reason of the disturbed condition of things, the purchasing power of the currency fluctuated greatly in brief intervals, the seller on all his time sales *bet* in favor of great risks, and *bet* differently every day, and added ten, fifteen, twenty, or even thirty per cent. to his prices over and above the general aggregate representing cost, profit, interest, and ordinary risk, in order to make sure of receiving currency of sufficient purchasing value to enable him to buy back as much gold as he was obliged to give for the cloth originally.

When, on the other hand, the fluctuations in the purchasing

power of the currency became limited, the insurance percentage added to price became also limited, and followed a somewhat general rule. Thus, when a clothing-dealer sold goods on *three months'* credit, for currency whose purchasing power was so much less than gold that it took one hundred and fifteen of currency to buy one hundred in gold, he added *five per cent.* to his sale price, or he bet that the depreciation of currency at the end of three months would be indicated by one hundred and twenty for gold; while for a credit longer than three months he bet that the risk of depreciation would be greater, and added, to cover this risk, an average of *ten per cent.* to his price. If now, at the end of *three* months, it required one hundred and twenty-five in currency to buy one hundred in gold, the dealer lost five per cent. through the payment of his debt. But if, on the other hand, the fluctuation of the purchasing power of the currency was the other way, and it required at the end of the three months only one hundred and ten of currency to buy a hundred in gold, he made ten per cent. over and above his ordinary and legitimate profit, while an equivalent burden or loss fell on the consumers.* As the dealers were shrewd, the result of this

---

* Although, to all who have investigated the subject, the evidence is conclusive that an irredeemable fluctuating paper money is always made an agency for taxing with special severity all that class of consumers who live on fixed incomes, salaries, and wages, it has, nevertheless, always been a somewhat difficult matter to find illustrations of the fact so clear and simple as carry conviction by presentation that it does thus act to the classes most interested. With a view of obtaining such an illustration, application was made some months since to an eminent American merchant, whose large and varied experience abundantly qualified him to discuss the subject; and the result of the application may be thus stated:

Q. In buying in gold and selling in currency, what addition do you make to your selling price, in the way of insurance, that the currency rebetting and insurance was rarely loss, and so constantly profit, that some dealers after a while came to regard the obtaining

---

ceived will be sufficient—plus profit, interest, etc.—to replace or buy back the gold represented by the original purchase?

A. We do but very little of that now; hardly enough to speak about.

Q. But still you make insurance against currency fluctuations an item in your business to be regarded to some extent?

A. Why, yes, certainly; it won't do to overlook it entirely.

Q. Well, then, if you have no objections, please tell me what you do allow under existing circumstances?

A. I have certainly no objections. We buy closely for cash; sell largely for cash, or very short credit; and, within the comparatively narrow limits that currency has fluctuated for the last two or three years, add but little to our selling prices as insurance on that account—say one to two per cent. for cash, or three months' credit; and for a longer credit—if we give it—something additional. During or immediately after the war, when the currency fluctuations were more extensive, frequent, and capricious, the case was very different. Then selling prices had to be watched very closely, and changed very frequently—sometimes daily. My present experience, therefore, is exceptional; and to get the information you want, you must look further. I think I can help you to do this. We buy regularly large quantities of a foreign product—let us suppose, for illustration, *cloth*, for the large manufacturers and dealers in ready-made clothing. We buy for gold, and we sell for gold, and do not allow the currency or its fluctuations to enter in any way into these transactions. But how is it with *my* customers? I allow them some credit; and the amount involved being often very large, I, of course, must know something of the way in which they manage their business. They transform the cloth, purchased with gold, into clothing; and then sell the clothing, in turn, to *their* customers—jobbers and retailers—all over the country, for currency, on a much longer average credit than they obtain from me for their raw material. As a matter of safety and necessity, these wholesale dealers and manufacturers must add to their selling prices a sufficient percentage to make sure that the currency they are to receive at the end of three, six, or nine months will be sufficient to buy them as much gold as they have paid to me, or as much as will buy them another lot of cloth to meet the of this species of profit as the main thing for which all business was instituted; while others, more clear-headed and discerning, concluded that the wisest and easiest way to get rich was to bet *directly* on the varying quantity of currency which it would take from day to day to buy the same quantity of gold, or other valuable commodities, instead of attempting to do the same thing indirectly, through the agency of stores,

---

further demands of their business and their customers. How much they thus add I can not definitely say. There is no regular rule. Every man doubtless adds all that competition will permit; and every circumstance likely to affect the prospective price of gold is carefully considered. Five per cent., in my opinion, on a credit of three months would be the average minimum; and for a longer time, a larger percentage. If competition does not allow any insurance percentage to be added, there is a liability to a loss of capital, which, in the long run, may be most disastrous—a circumstance that may explain the wreck of many firms, whose managers, on the old-fashioned basis of doing business, would have been successful. The jobbers and the retailers, to whom the wholesale dealers and manufacturers sell, are not so likely to take currency insurance into consideration in fixing their selling prices; but to whatever amount the cost price of their goods has been enhanced by the necessity of insurance against currency fluctuations, on that same amount they estimate and add for interest and profits; the total enhancement of prices falling ultimately on the consumer, who, of necessity, can rarely know the elements of the cost of the article he purchases.

Q. So Mr. Webster, then, in his remark, which has become almost a proverb, that "of all contrivances for cheating the laboring classes, none has been more effectual than that which deludes them with paper money," must have been thoroughly cognizant of the nature of such transactions?

A. Most undoubtedly; for such transactions are the inevitable consequence of using as a medium of exchange a variable, irredeemable currency.

The illustration above given, therefore, in the place of being imaginary, is based on the actual condition of business at the present time—January, 1876.

ONE WAY OF BLOWING A DISSATISFIED PARTY OUT OF EXISTENCE.

stocks of goods, clerks, books, credits, and the like. The
last, accordingly, wound up their business, and, in the language of the day, "*went on to the street*," and made their
living by selling on time what they did not possess, and buying on time what they never expected to receive, and reckon-
ing profit or loss according to the difference in prices grow-

ing out of the fluctuations of the currency between the day of buying or selling, and the day of receiving or delivering. In short, as with the magic fiddle in the fairy tale, which, when played upon, made every body dance, no matter whether in the brambles or on the plain, so the use on the island of a currency which continually fluctuated in purchasing power, because it was not a constant equivalent of any thing, made every body gamble that could; some because they liked to, and others because they had to, to protect themselves from losses. The masses who could not conveniently gamble tried to protect themselves by asking high prices in return for their services, or by giving less in proportion to what they received;* but, in the long run, they learned by hard experience that they were not as well off as they expected to be; and that if one effect of an overabundant, non-equivalent-to-any-thing currency was to stimulate production, another and greater effect of it was to unequally distribute the results of production, transferring from those who had little to those who had much, and thus making the rich richer, and the poor poorer.

---

* In 1864, a ship was built in New York, at the time when labor and materials, reckoned in currency, had touched their highest prices. In 1870, another ship was built in the same place and on the same model—like the former in every particular. It was expected that, as wages and the cost of materials were less in 1870 than in 1864, the cost of the latter ship would be much less than that of the former; but the result showed that this was not the case.

✓

CHAPTER X.

AFTER THE WAR.

AT last the war ended. The cannibals were utterly repulsed; and the islanders no longer laid awake nights for fear of being roasted and eaten. A vast amount of every thing useful had, however, been necessarily destroyed; and it would seem as if this admitted fact would have made the people of the island feel poor. But, very curiously, it did not. The promises to pay for the commodities destroyed had all been preserved. They were regarded by almost every body as money; and if money, then, of course, as every body knew, they were wealth, and wealth so great and superabundant that the one thing especially necessary to do was to devise plans for using it. Every body, therefore, devised plans; those who had no money more especially devising plans for those who had. All sorts of schemes were accordingly entered upon; railroads to carry people to the isothermals and every other place where they didn't want to go; and oil-wells on Cheat and Al(l)gon(e)quin rivers, and patented inventions for making substitutes for tea and coffee, being especially recommended as permanent investments. John Law, Lemuel Gulliver, Baron Munchausen, Sir John Mandeville, Juan Ferdinand Mendez-Pinto, and Sindbad the Sailor, all came to town, and were chronicled in the newspapers as having registered at the principal hotels.

Great and commendable industry was also displayed in replacing the things destroyed by the war, so that, for a time,

AFTER THE WAR.73

the societary circulation became more brisk than ever; while
some who had up to this time regarded war as a misfortune
and national calamity, now felt that they had made a mistake;
and others who had known all the time that war was a blessing, seriously thought of proposing another war as a means of
increasing national prosperity.* The large and constant in-
vestment of the results of labor and economy in enterprises
which never could by any possibility give back any adequate
return, was, as every body saw, the next best thing to war; and
on the advice of the most Christian newspapers, very many of
the best people made haste to make such use of their little
savings; although, as agriculturists, they were perfectly well
aware that to plant seed wheat or corn in soils where it
would not come up, or, coming up, bear no fruit, was always
very bad business, and did not encourage the sower to hire
much additional labor the next year.

Another idea which about this time had become very popular on the island was, that while it was a very desirable thing
to sell as much as possible of the products of the island to people in other countries, it was not desirable to buy any thing
from foreigners in return, and that it was wise to put all possible obstructions in the way of any ill-informed persons who
desired to make such exchanges. But as no one can long continue to buy unless he proportionally sells, or sell unless he
proportionally buys, the foreign commerce of the island soon
came to a stand-still; and what also notably helped to this
result was, that the necessity of insuring all exchanges made
through the medium of the unstable currency of the island

* When the Japanese embassy visited the United States, in 1872, they
were seriously advised to create, by some means, a national debt as soon
as they returned home, and make use of it as a basis for the creation and
issue of currency.

caused all the island products to cost from *five* to *ten* or *fifteen* per cent. more than they otherwise would, and more than they would cost the foreigners to buy elsewhere.* But as every industrious community (especially if it calls in the aid of the forces of nature through machinery) produces more than it consumes; and as the islanders were both industrious and ingenious, it oddly enough happened that the community became sorely troubled by an accumulation of useful things, which the manufacturers would not part with, because they were unwilling to sell at a loss, and which the foreigners would not buy because they could buy cheaper elsewhere, and pay in their own products for what they bought. Then the manufacturers stopped producing, and next the laborers, by lack of employment, being unable to buy a full share of the existing abundance, in turn diminished their consumption; so that for a time it seemed as though the island would get into the condition of those unfortunate people who die of their own fatness.

In this way the times gradually "got out of joint." Gradually the people on the island came to realize that much which they had considered as wealth was not wealth, and that many influences, before little regarded, were powerfully act-

---

* Machiavelli, in his "Discourses on the First Ten Books of Livy," book ii., chap. iii., in explaining the great difference in the relative growth of the Roman and Spartan republics, relates that "Lycurgus, the founder of the Spartan republic, believing that nothing could more readily destroy his laws than the admixture of new inhabitants, did every thing possible to deter strangers from flocking thither. Besides denying them intermarriage, citizenship, and all other companionships (*conversationi*) that bring men together, *he ordered that in his republic only leather* (non-exportable) *money should be used, so as to indispose all strangers to bring merchandise into Sparta, or to exercise any kind of art or industry there, so that the city never could increase in population.*"

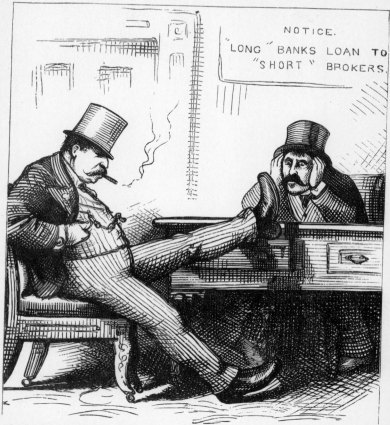

THIS SCHEME ACCORDINGLY FOUND MANY OPPONENTS, WHO ALLEGED THAT, IF IT WERE CARRIED OUT, IT WOULD DEPRIVE THEM OF MONEY, AND CONSEQUENTLY OF INSTRUMENTALITIES FOR MAKING THEIR EXCHANGES.

ing to make and keep them poor. All were satisfied that the currency which they were using was one prime cause of their difficulties, but in precisely what manner the currency exerted an influence few agreed. All were of one mind, that they ought to talk about it continually; and they accordingly did so, those who knew the least talking the most. Some thought that the honest thing to do, and because honest the best, was for the Government of the island to redeem its promises to pay on demand as rapidly as possible; that where they had borrowed a canoe of one man, cloth of another, spears of a third, or money of a fourth, they should return them, and not keep promising and never doing. But even these did not agree as to the manner of thus paying. Some thought it was best to return the canoes, the iron, the cloth, and the money from day to day as the Government gradually acquired them. Others thought that a better way would be to accumulate each separate thing in a separate warehouse, and then when the warehouses had, after some years, become full, open the doors, and return every man what had been borrowed of him all at once. But, as before pointed out, the Government never had, or could have, any canoes, cloth, iron, or money, except such as it obtained from the people; and, therefore, payment on the part of the Government was really the same thing as payment on the part of the people. But payment of debts is something to which many people are constitutionally opposed; and this scheme accordingly found many opponents, who alleged that, if it were carried out, it would deprive them of money, and consequently of instrumentalities for making their exchanges; while the real trouble with many of this class of people was, that they hadn't any thing useful, the products of their own industry, *to exchange*, and therefore could get no money, unless they went to work, or, what was preferable, acquired it from somebody without consideration.

Besides the persons referred to, who either openly or by their indecision opposed fiscal reform, there were various other classes of obstructives. There were those, for example, who, during the war, were always friends of peace, dressed in broad-brimmed hats and drab coats, and were at any time ready to compromise with the cannibals, on condition that the latter should be satisfied with roasting and eating only the old men, the babies, and an occasional mother-in-law. All such, as a part of their peace policy, opposed the original issue and circulation of the bluebacks as something arbitrary, illegal, and unnecessary. When, however, the cannibals were driven away, these "friends of peace in time of war" at once changed their Quaker garb; became "friends of war in time of peace;" declared earnestly for the enlarged issue and continued use of the bluebacks, and, as a pretext for so doing, were willing, if necessary, to have another war, or, at least, an annual scare. During the war, these friends of peace were called "copper-heads;" and after the war, their copper-head-ism, although disguised, was substantially the same thing. For it was apparent that opposition to the issue of the blue-backs, as manifested by the advocates of peace during the war, and opposition to their payment and withdrawal after the war, were only different manifestations of hostility to the Government and to the war itself: inasmuch as failure on the part of the Government to observe its promises, made under such circumstances of extreme peril, would manifestly put it in bad repute, and prevent it from ever resorting to similar measures in like emergencies.* The really intelligent and patriotic men of the island at once saw through this duplicity

---

* Examination will show that the United States, for one-sixth part of their existence as a federated nation, have been in a state of war; and, for the future, there is no good reason for supposing that the country is to be any more exempt from the vicissitudes of nations than it has been in the past. With irredeemable paper, violation of plighted faith, gold de-monetized and banished, in what condition is the nation for maintaining a great national struggle?

and repudiation, advocated under pretense of extreme solicitude for the wants of trade.   They remembered the old couplet :

" When the devil was sick, the devil a monk would be ;
*When the devil got well, the devil a monk was he ;"**

and thereafter designated the opponents of paying the blue-backs, as inflated, or elongated, copper-heads, by which name they were ever after known in history.

There were also many well-meaning citizens, who sincerely desired to have the balloon of inflation come down, but strenuously objected to have this result effected by any diminution of the volume of gas contained in it.   All the first-cousins of the man who waited for the river to run by before crossing were certain the balloon would come down, if people would only be patient, keep a sharp lookout, and wait.   But to this it was objected, that if people were obliged to consume a large part of their time in watching the balloon, to avoid having their heads smashed by its swayings and fluctuations, there would ultimately be a scarcity of victuals and drink ; and that, rendered desperate with watching, and want of employment, food, and clothing, those interested would finally insist on pulling open the valves, and letting the whole volume of gas escape at once.   Some proposed to imitate the example of "Peter the Headstrong" in fighting the Yankees, and bring down the balloon by proclamation ; while others professed to have great faith in family prayer.   Eminent patriotic constitutional lawyers maintained that the military necessity that authorized and created the bluebacks must necessarily limit their duration solely to the period of their military

---

* In a case often overlooked (Bank *vs.* Supervisors, 7 Wallace), the United States Supreme Court decided that *"United States notes are engagements to pay dollars ; and the dollars intended are coined dollars of the United States."*   Refusal to pay such notes in coin is clearly, therefore, repudiation.

necessity; and that their continued re-issue and use after the repulse of the cannibals was but a prolongation of the war—not against the enemy, but against their own people. The astute elongated copper-head lawyers held, on the other hand, that an instrument of military necessity, once created, remains such an instrumentality for continued use for all time; and, therefore, that a bullet or shell, once lawfully employed for effecting destruction in time of war, could legitimately be re-issued or reshot in time of peace, without matter as to whom it might hit or what property it might destroy; and that, in fact, to go on reloading and refiring these instruments, and thereby killing and destroying, were not crimes, but high acts of patriotism. This theory, however, alarmed some timid people, who said that one shell or one bullet thus re-used indefinitely might destroy all the property, or kill all the people on the island; and they rather regretted, in view of such a construction, that they did not at once succumb to the cannibals, whose appetites, in time, might have become cloyed, or whose diet might have been changed through indigestion or moral suasion.

In the period of doubt and perplexity which thus came to the community, those fond of precedents carefully searched the old chronicles and records of other nations for lessons of experience; and, among various things which profited them greatly, they found, among the chronicles of the learned Spanish historian, Fray Antonio Agapida, the following account of what the veteran soldier, Don Inigo Lopez de Mendoza, Count de Tendilla, did, when, besieged by the Moors in the town of Alhama, he had also serious financial difficulties to contend with:

"It happened," says Agapida, "that this Catholic cavalier, at one time, was destitute of gold and silver wherewith to pay the wages of his troops; and the soldiers murmured greatly, seeing that they had not the means of purchasing necessities from the people of the town. In this dilemma, what does this most sagacious commander? He takes me a number of little morsels of paper, on the which he inscribes various sums, large and small, according to the nature of the case, and signs me them with his own hand and name. These did he give to the soldiery, in earnest of their pay. 'How!' you will say, 'are soldiers to be paid with scraps of paper?' 'Even so,' I answer, 'and well paid, too, as I will presently make manifest; for the good count issued a proclamation ordering the inhabitants of Alhama to take these morsels of paper for the full amount thereon inscribed, promising to redeem them at a future time with silver and gold, and threatening severe punishment to all who should refuse. The people, having full confidence in his word, and trusting that he would be as willing to perform the one promise as he certainly was able to perform the other, took these curious morsels of paper without hesitation or demur. Thus, by a subtile and most miraculous kind of alchemy, did this Catholic cavalier turn worthless paper into precious gold, and make his late impoverished garrison abound in money!'

"It is but just to add," continues the historian, "that the Count de Tendilla redeemed his promises, like a loyal knight; and this miracle, as it appeared in the eyes of Agapida, is the first instance on record of paper money."*

It may be also remarked that the island antiquarians did not find any chronicle of any other soldier who imitated Count de Tendilla in issuing "little morsels of paper" to serve as money, and subsequently did not imitate him in promptly redeem-

* Irving's "Conquest of Granada."

"AN INSTRUMENT OF MILITARY NECESSITY, ONCE CREATED, REMAINS SUCH AN
INSTRUMENTALITY FOR CONTINUED USE FOR ALL TIME; NO MATTER WHO
IT MAY HIT, OR WHAT PROPERTY IT MAY DESTROY."

6

ing his promises, who found it easy to obtain again the confidence of the soldiers or the people when he again got into similar difficulties.*

CHAPTER XI.

THE NEW MILLENNIUM.

At last there arose a sect of philosophers (calling themselves Friends of Humanity) who felt confident of settling all difficulties, and who also aspired to the government of the island.

Their chief had the reputation of being an ogre. He had served in the war against the cannibals, looked exceedingly fierce, and therefore was accounted brave; he talked loud and with great assurance, and therefore he was accounted wise; he had acquired great riches without ever doing any thing useful, and therefore he was accounted skilled in business.

His principal associates and counselors were two. The first was a great orator, who had spent most of his life as a missionary among an uneducated people who never had any property, and, of course, made no exchanges; and in this most excellent and practical school had learned all that could be acquired on this complicated subject. The second was a great athlete, who had performed for many years in the national cir-

---

* In every cabinet of rare coins in Europe there will be found specimens of what are known as *"obsidional"* coins, or coins struck in besieged places to supply the place of coined money. These coins appear, in all instances, to have been regarded as obligations sacred in their nature, and their repudiation a high crime against morality and patriotism.

cus, and had acquired great reputation by carrying weighty packages on both shoulders, labeled "domestic industry," but which in reality contained only pig-iron. About these two "every one that was in distress, every one that was in debt, and every one that was discontented gathered themselves," so that they soon had a large body of disciples.

The first thing they did was to abuse poor old Robinson Crusoe, because he had advised his people, in his life-time, to make their money of gold (which can be only produced by labor, and not by hocus-pocus); and their currency of something that represented gold, and this, too, when he must have known that gold "was the machinery and relic of old despotisms;"* and they made no account whatever of the fact that he was the father of his country and lived in a cave. Next they declared that all the opinions heretofore accepted on this subject by the rest of mankind were fallacious; that nature had done its best to make the island an isolated community; that legislation had pretty effectually supplemented whatever in this respect nature had left deficient; and, therefore, that the wants of the island, in respect to money, currency, and every thing else, were so exceptional and peculiar that the accumulated experience of all the rest of the world could not be to them either applicable or instructive. All agreed that the pernicious theory taught by Robinson Crusoe, Friday, and other men of by-gone days and other countries— that money, to be good, ought to be a universally desirable commodity, and the equivalent of that for which it is exchanged—was the real source of all financial trouble; for was it not clear, that, if such were the case, those only could ever have money who, like the bloated wheat-holders, pig-

---

* Speech of General B. F. Butler, United States House of Representatives.

THE DOCTORS PRESCRIBE CONTINUED LOW (FISCAL) DIET.

holders, cattle-holders, house-holders, or bond-holders, had through labor previously come into possession of some desirable things, which they could give in exchange as an equivalent for money? while the true end of all financial reform, and the key to the terrible problem of poverty, was obviously to devise and bring into use that kind of money which those who had no wheat, pigs, cattle, houses, bonds, or other commodities, and were not able or disposed to acquire any through an exchange of their services, could have without difficulty, and in abundance. "We mean, therefore," said the orator-philosopher, speaking for himself and his colleague Friends of Humanity, "to have more democracy and less aristocracy in the money market; more money in every body's reach, and less for the petted few."* In short, the patient having become very sick and attenuated by reason of the low (fiscal) diet upon which he had been fed, the doctors now proposed to resuscitate him by administering a still thinner gruel.

All also agreed that the word "money" was a bad name, and that the public would obtain a much clearer idea of the great problems at issue if more intelligible and scientific terms embodying definitions were used. One philosopher accordingly proposed that, as they intended to sprout it everywhere, they should go back to the Biblical designation, and call it the "root," at the same time remarking that "the Lord showed what he thought of money by the kind of people he gave it to." Another proposed to call it "the instrument of association" (Carey); a third, the "sign of transmission, of which the material shall be of native growth" (John Law, 1705); a fourth, "a sense of value as compared with commodities" ("British Tracts on Money," 1795–1810); a fifth, "a standard neither gold nor silver, but something set up in the imagination to be regulated by public opinion" (*ibid.*).

As to what money, under the reform system, was, or should be, was also a question in respect to which there was not at first an entire agreement. One idea which found some favor, was, that money ought to be only a token, representative of

---

* Letter of Wendell Phillips to the New York Legal-tender Club, 1875.

services rendered at some indefinite time or place (possibly forgotten or disputed by its recipient), and "for which the holder has not received the equivalent to which he is inherently entitled under the system of division of labor."* The best money, therefore, according to the philosophers of this idea, was an evidence that some one person owed some other person; and, consequently, the more debt, the more money; and the more money, the more wealth, unless it is to be supposed (as is not reasonable) that this sort of money was not to have the first attribute of all other money—namely, purchasing power.

Moreover, although the philosophers did not exactly say so, the inference was also legitimate, that in a community using merely "token" or "remembrance" money, the surest way to get rich would be to get in debt, and the best way of carrying on an enlightened system of trade and commerce, to exchange commodities, the results of time and labor, for evidences of debt without interest. It is needless to say that these teachings and inferences tended to greatly strengthen the people on the island in the opinion they before entertained, that the currency they already had—namely, evidences of destruction— was the "best currency the world ever saw."

The three leaders among the philosophers were not, however, men who were going to be contented with any half-way measures. Had they not put their hands to the plow of reform? and were they, after so doing, to allow the plow to stick fast in the furrow? They accordingly appealed first to authority, and then to untutored reason.

The following are some of the authorities to which great weight was given:

---

* Charles Moran, *New York Commercial Bulletin,* October 5th, 1875.

"Commerce and population, which are the riches and power of the state, depend on the quantity and management of money.—JOHN LAW, *Memoir to the Duke of Orleans*, 1705.

"Does, or does not, our duty to ourselves and the world at large demand that we maintain permanently a non-exportable circulation? Such is the question which now agitates the nation, and must at no distant day absorb all others. The affirmative of this question is also in perfect harmony with the practice and experience of leading nations, and in harmony with the teachings of sound economic science."—*Letter of Henry C. Carey to Congressman Moses W. Field, of Detroit*, September, 1875. Consult also Governor William Kieft, "On the Use of Wampum Money in New Amsterdam" (large folio, scarce and rare), 1659.

"Long familiarity with the practice of giving security for loans, and of paying them back at a fixed date, has blinded us to the national advantages of loans without security and payable at any date."—KARL MARX, *Sécrétaire, Organisation de l'Internationale.*

But the thing which the philosophers relied on more than any thing else to sustain their views before the people was a judicial decision recently made in a neighboring country, by its highest court, before whom the question as to what constituted money was officially brought for determination. This decision, expressed in the very peculiar language of the country, was as follows: "What we do assert is, that Congress has power to enact that the Government promises to pay money *shall be*, for the time being, equivalent in value to the representative of value determined by the coinage acts, or to multiples thereof." All of which, translated into the language of the island, meant that Government has the power to make a promise to pay, containing an acknowledgment in itself that the promise has not been paid, a full satisfaction that the promise has been paid. That this decision, furthermore, covered no new points of law, was indirectly conceded by the learned judges, inasmuch as, in giving their opinions, they cited, as precedents worthy of being ever remembered, the decisions of that eminent old-time jurist, Cade (Jack), who ordained that "seven half-penny loaves should be sold for a penny;" and that "the three-hooped pot shall have ten hoops." The same court also strengthened its position by saying that "it is hardly correct to speak of a standard of value. The Constitution does not speak of it. Value is an *ideal* thing. The coinage acts fix its unit as a dollar; but the gold and silver thing we call a dollar is in no sense the standard of a dollar. It is a representative of it. There might never have been a piece of money of the denomination of a dollar."*

[NOTE.—This last remark of the learned court embodied a great discovery; for how can there be a representative without something to represent? In the case of Peter Schlemihl, there was a man without a shadow; but here we have a shadow without any substance to make it. A gold dollar is not a specific and mechanically formed coin; but 25.8 grains of standard gold is a dollar. Did the court mean that these grains of gold may never have existed, and yet have representatives?—*Author*.]

The moment this decision was received, all the philosophers got down their dictionaries, and searched for the meaning of the word "*ideal*." As was anticipated, its definition was found to be "visionary;" "existing in fancy or imagination only" (Webster); and from this time forth there was no longer any doubt in the minds of the reformers of the truth and strength of the position they occupied. For, to descend to reasoning, were not two intricate questions definitely settled by the highest of human tribunals? 1st. That the representative of a thing may be (and if those in authority say so, shall be) equiv-

---

* Opinion of the United States Supreme Court, by Justice Strong.— WALLACE, 12, p. 553.

alent to the thing itself. 2d. That value is an ideal thing, and therefore imagination, which creates all ideal things, can create value.

It followed, of course, that to have and enjoy any thing and every thing, it is only necessary to create and use its symbol or representative; and to pay for value received, it is only necessary to imagine a corresponding and equivalent value, and pass it over in exchange and settlement. On these conclusions of law and reason, then, it was decided by the three leaders of the philosophers and their friends, who had control of the Government, that the future money of the state should be based. The former inscription on the currency in use, "promise to pay," they were clear, was entirely unnecessary; for why promise money when the store on hand of money was to be made practically unlimited, or, at least, always equal to the wants of every body who desired to have it, whether he traded or not? Mathematical calculations were also made by a scientist, which proved that the amount of labor which would be actually saved to the community, and made available for other purposes, by using something as money which cost little or no labor to produce, in place of gold or commodities which represented much labor, would be so great as to require the immediate enactment of a law prohibiting any one from working over six hours per day, in order to guard against the evil of too great abundance. The same scientist had previously been so carried away by his demonstrations of the utility of a new stove which saved half the fuel, that he had recommended the purchase of two stoves in order to save the whole.

With few exceptions, to be hereafter noted, the whole population of the island were jubilant, and proceeded as rapidly as circumstances would permit to adjust all their commercial transactions to the new basis. But joy at the prospect of the coming millennium did not extinguish feelings of gratitude in the hearts of the people, and they resolved to send ample testimonials to all, in foreign lands, to whom they had been indebted for wisdom.

To each of the judges who had so intelligently defined value they accordingly voted an ideal castle and estate, possession of the same conferring nobility upon their owner, with the title of "*Baron Ideality*," to which, by special patent, the recipient was authorized to use (if he pleased) the prefix of "*damn*."

To the most notable advocate, in foreign lands, of the idea of non-exportable money a gift of one million of "instruments of association," represented by ideal currency, was voted. But as this currency, both by law and the fitness of things, could not be exported from the island, it became impossible to pay this gift, and in its place a letter was written explaining the circumstances, and requesting that the resolution to pay might be accepted as a "sign of transmission."

To the eminent financier who defined money, "as a sense of value in reference to currency as compared with commodities," there was sent a plaster image of the "*What Is It;*" while to his colleague, who had given the opinion that "the less costly the material out of which money was made, the better for the community which uses it," was sent a large box, containing contributions of the most worthless things every body could think of, with a polite note requesting the recipient to make his choice out of the collection of what seemed to him best adapted as a token, and forward a detailed report of his experience in attempting to use it as a representative of unrequited service.

Pending the slow preparations of the Government of the isl-

THE ARAB AND THE CAMEL.

An Arab asked the loaded camel whether he preferred to go up or down hill. "Pray, master," said the camel, dryly, "is the *straight* way across the plain shut up?"—*Æsop.*

and to provide the requisite laws for the issue and use of the new money, various enlightened individuals attempted to anticipate official legislative action by putting into practical operation, on their own account, the principles involved in the new fiscal system. The first of these who thus acted was a secretary for the interior part of the island, whose chief business was to supply the heathen—for whom, it will be remembered, Robinson Crusoe took up contributions—with beef. There had been a suspicion for some time past hanging over this official that the heathen did not get all the beef that they were entitled to; but the suspicion probably had no further foundation than the inability of the heathen to make the sense of completion harmonize with the sign of transmission. To satisfy the heathen, and at the same time effectually clear up his character, the official in question now hastened to have prepared a large number of pictures of fine, fat cattle, which he dispatched by a Quaker to the heathen, with a request that they would kill and eat, and be satisfied, adding in a postscript that they would do well to begin to learn economy by saving the skins. As the Quaker never came back, it was deemed reasonably certain that, at least, the first part of the request had been complied with.

The managers of the Island Provident Society also promptly determined to develop and apply the ideal system in their sphere of usefulness to the full extent that circumstances permitted. Thus a large part of the business of this old and respected society was the distribution of clothing to the destitute; and, as is always the case when times are hard, the extent of the demands made upon it for aid tended to exceed the means of supply contributed by the charitable. The managers, however, knew that it never would answer in using the ideal system to subserve the work of charity, to put the locally needy on the same footing as the heathen, and in answer to appeals for raiment distribute to them elaborate pictures of fine clothing, cut from the fashion-plates; for there was this essential difference in the situations, that the needy were at their doors, while the heathen were a great way off. They, therefore, hit upon this happy mean: they employed a com-

petent artist, with a full supply of paints and brushes, and
when any destitute person applied for clothing, they painted
upon his person every thing he desired in way of clothing of
the finest and most fashionable patterns, from top-boots to
collars, and from blue swallow-tailed coats to embroidered
neck-ties, with jewelry and fancy buttons to match. Of course,
the first man who appeared in public thus arrayed created a
profound sensation. But the idea was so novel, and had obviously so many advantages over the old way of clothing one's
self, that the supremacy of the ideal over the real was at once
greatly strengthened. For example—and here was one of the
greatest merits of the new system—it not only symbolized,
but practically applied, the views of the most advanced financial philosophers; favored (as the orator-philosopher wished)
"more democracy and less aristocracy in the clothes market;"
and encouraged the use of the least costly material out of which
the community could make clothes; while the painted cotton,
silk, wool, and leather could be made to look so exactly like
the real articles, that it was only when the attempt was made
to exchange the representative for the real that the difference was clearly discernible. Furthermore, every garment
devised in accordance with the new system was, in all cases,
a perfect fit. The plague of buttons was annihilated. Every
man could save time enough in dressing and undressing to
enrich himself, if he only employed his economized moments
usefully. Every man might, without embarrassment, sleep in
his clothes; and if he desired to change his monkey-jacket
three hundred and sixty-five times in a year for an overcoat,
or an overcoat for a monkey-jacket, he could do it most expe-
ditiously, without the waste of any raw material more expen-
sive than paint; and thus the system, after a time, by a happy
thought, got the name of the "*three-sixty-five interchangea-*

ble." Of course, this answered very well so long as the weather continued mild and pleasant; but later in the season, when it became cool and frosty, experience soon showed that the warming qualities of different kinds of paint were not essentially different; that something more than confidence was necessary to keep out the cold; and that the temperature and circulation of the body physical remained unaffected, whether a man painted himself sky-blue one day and pea-green the next.*

Again, two shrewd fellows, Peter von Scrapehem and Israel Double, owned each a farm worth ten thousand dollars. Peter sold his farm for its full value to Israel, and took a mortgage for the total purchase-money; and Israel, in turn, sold his to Peter, and took a mortgage also for its full value. By so doing, each of these worthy persons clearly doubled the property in his possession, inasmuch as while each had at the outset only ten thousand dollars' worth of real estate, each now had ten thousand of real estate and ten thousand of personal property; or an aggregate of forty thousand between them, in the place of twenty thousand originally. This method of multiplying property by multiplying titles was so easy, and the result so apparent, that the example was very generally followed; and when the census came to be taken, a few months afterward, all were amazed at the enormous increase of wealth that had followed the discovery and simple recognition of the true nature and value of titles.

---

* The Indians on the Atrato River (Central America), when first visited by one of the recent inter-ocean-canal exploring parties, were found to be unaccustomed to the use of much, if any, clothing; but after a little intercourse with civilized man, some of the more intelligent of the natives presented themselves with their bodies painted in close imitation of clothes, which they claimed to be superior in every respect to the genuine articles worn by their visitors.

Up to this time the supply of milk on the island had been mainly controlled by a single corporation, which, under the name of the "Lacteal Fluid Association," owned all the cows, and, for the purpose of facilitating supply, had long been in the habit of issuing tickets, each good for a pint or a quart of milk, and disposing of milk to those only who had tickets. These tickets revolved perfectly in the closed circle of exchange between the milk-men and their customers, satisfying all demands, and being accepted as the same thing as milk; for the more tickets, the more milk; and no tickets, no milk.

During the war the cannibals, in lack of any other meat, had eaten a large number of the cows belonging to the "Lacteal Association." Many had been also taken by the Government for the soldiers; so that after the war was over there were really no more cows than the island absolutely needed. All at once, the "foot-and-mouth disease" invaded the island, and, attacking every cow belonging to the association, rendered her unable to give milk. Then arose such a piteous cry from every household where there were babies as carried a pang to the stoutest hearts. There was no need of any concerted action, for the people assembled spontaneously and demanded action. An immense public meeting was at once organized. A highly popular and humane man, a special friend of children, familiarly known as Uncle Dick, was called to the chair. He was supported by a long list of leading citizens as vice-presidents and secretaries, none of whom, however, had had any practical acquaintance with milk since their childhood, except in the form of punch. The chairman made an eloquent speech. He did not know whether he was most agitated by pity or indignation—pity for the poor babies, whose sufferings had become intolerable; indignation at the cruelty of the chartered monopolists, who had wantonly refused to is-

MILK-TICKETS FOR BABIES, IN PLACE OF MILK.

7

sue more tickets at the very time when the demand for milk was most imperative. The assembly was of one mind with the chairman, and unanimously resolved that the Lacteal Association should immediately increase their supply of tickets, and that, in default thereof, their charter should be altered and amended. Unable to resist the storm of popular indignation, the association at once complied, and every patriotic citizen went home to the bosom of his afflicted family, carrying an abundant supply of milk-tickets, and feeling conscious that for once at least he had risen to the level of the occasion.

That night the babies were all supplied with milk-tickets in the place of milk. Milk-tickets hot, milk-tickets cold, milk-tickets sweetened, milk-tickets plain, milk-tickets with their backs printed green, and interchangeable with milk-tickets drawing cream skimmed from other milk-tickets. But, strange to say, the babies, one and all, with that same sort of instinctive perversity which induces children of a larger growth to refuse to accept shams for reality, and be grateful in addition, refused to take to milk-tickets. The uproar of the night preceding was as nothing to the disturbances of the night following, and morning dawned upon an unrefreshed and troubled population.

As soon as the necessary arrangements could be made, another meeting assembled. But the meeting this time was composed of babies, backed by their mammas and nurses. There was no theory in their sentiments; and though young in years, one and all felt that they had lived long enough to know what their fathers apparently did not know—namely, the difference between milk and paper. The resolutions voted were brief, but to the point, and were, substantially, as follows:

First, that the exigencies of the times demanded more milk, and not more milk-tickets; *second*, that the way to get more

milk was to have more cows; *third*, that the way to get more
cows was to go to work and raise them, or raise something
else equally valuable, and then with this something else buy
cows; *fourth*, that there are certain eternal verities against
which it is useless for either babies or men to contend. A
committee was appointed to procure a mill of the gods, to
grind up those who disbelieved in the last resolution, and the
meeting then adjourned.

This was the first indication of any thing like popular dis-
sent from the views of the Friends of Humanity. Others,
however, soon followed. Value having been declared to be an
ideal thing, and ideal measures of value having been substituted in the place of the real and tangible measures formerly
in use, it had been deemed proper to substitute ideal measures
of length, weight, and capacity in the place of the foot-rules,
yard-sticks, pound-weights, and bushel-measures formerly employed. Shop-keepers, plumbers, charcoal - men, gas corpora-
tors, and all others who had any thing to sell accordingly provided themselves with slips of paper, upon which were printed, respectively, "This is a foot," "This is a bushel," "This is
a pint," "This is a pound;" and the services of the arithme-
tic-man were again called for, to prove how much more cloth,
beer, charcoal, gas, and all other measurable things the community would certainly have by the saving of labor and capital contingent on the avoidance of the necessity of further
manufacturing, purchasing, and using the old measures.

But the new system did not work smoothly. There was no
harmony of sentiment between buyers and sellers; and what
was one man's ideal of what he should give or receive in trade
was always different from every other man's; and, before the
community were well aware of what they were about, they
found themselves drifting back to the adoption of the old sys-

tem of barter, which had been tried and abandoned in the early days of the island's history. Instead of one price, every one who had commodities or services to sell adopted a scale of at least four prices: "pay price," "money price," "pay as money price," and a "trusting price;" and the seller, before fixing his price, invariably asked his customer how he would pay.* "Pay price" was barter; "money price" was payment in foreign coin; "pay as money" was in the ideal money of the island; "trusting" was an enhanced price, according to time. Thus, supposing a customer wanted a knife, its price in "pay" would be a bushel of corn; in "money price," a fifty-cent gold or silver coin; in "pay as money," sometimes as much as he could bring in a basket, at other times as much as he could bring in a wheelbarrow; and before the ultimate abandonment of the use of ideal money, a cart had to be employed to bring the money. Trade in this way became "most intricate."

News also came, about this time, that the heathen, not being able to stay their stomachs with the pictures of fat cattle that had been so abundantly sent them, and considering themselves humbugged, were preparing to declare war. To meet a threatened increased expenditure on this account, the Government, therefore, levied new taxes; and as the valuation of the property of the island, under the influence of the new fiscal system, had, as before stated, enormously increased, it was anticipated that a small rate would yield a large revenue. But as soon as Scrapehem, Double, and their friends, who had been multiplying their property by multiplying titles, found

---

* This was what actually happened in Connecticut in 1704 and thereabouts. See "Madame Knight's Journal," quoted in Felt and Bronson's "Histories of New England Currencies."

AN INFLATION LOOK AHEAD.

out that the titles were to be valued and assessed as wealth, equally with the property which the titles represented, they hasted to swap back, and cancel their mortgages; and immediately half the reputed wealth of the island disappeared.

There were some people, it will be remembered, who did not share in the general jubilation which welcomed the discovery and adoption of the new monetary system. These were the stony-hearted capitalists, meaning thereby persons who had produced by industry and frugality more than they had consumed, and had lent out this surplus in the form of ships, houses, horses and carts, wheelbarrows, coal, iron, and the like, on condition that they should be repaid the value of the several articles as expressed in money, with a portion of the profit that might have accrued to the borrower from their using.

There was a popular feeling that all these lenders were "bloated," the degrees of bloat being, of course, different all the way from the man who owned and lent a ship down to the man who owned and lent a cart, or their equivalents in money; and that the best remedy for this frightful disease was tapping, and tapping by tendering in payment the ideal money, which was something very different in value from the money understood at the time the loans were effected. Natives of heathen lands, who had never enjoyed the light of the Gospel, called this robbing; but many on the island who had always been Christians regarded the matter with indifference, and treated it as a purely sanitary measure; and Christian ministers who never preached against such practices, but always did preach against the sins of that ancient people, the Jews, wondered at the low tone of morality that seemed to generally characterize society. As it appears, however, from an examination of the ancient records of the island, that strenuous exertions were made about this time to interest the Government and the people in the momentous question of the reading of the Bible in the public schools, and thus prevent public attention from being diverted to the consideration of any such unimportant and side issues as the nature and obligations of promises, it may be that the low tone of morality thus referred to was more apparent than real; no province devolving upon the historian being more difficult than that of attempting to reconcile, after a long lapse of years, what appears to be a series of contemporaneous but utterly incongruous circumstances.

But, be this as it may, all who had loaned valuable commodities desired to avoid tapping, and consequently hastened to demand repayment before the ideal money could be extensively issued and put into circulation; and, having once obtained payment, were very cautious how they lent again. All this contributed, in the language of the day, to make money very tight; but this language had, to a great extent, no meaning. The only money that was tight was good money, and this had been gone so long that the younger part of the population didn't even know how it looked; while of the bad money there was a continually increasing quantity.

Besides good money, all real capital, timber for building ships, factories, and houses, iron for the construction of machinery, cloth for clothes, and grain for food, were tight; not because there was any lack of all these useful things, but because the owners had all become afraid that if they once loaned or parted with them they should never receive back an equivalent. So the island, instead of being lifted up to great prosperity, was plunged into the depths of adversity. There was a general lack of confidence. Societary activity was abated; production was arrested; and men desirous of being industrious had no opportunity of following any industry.

Gold had long disappeared from circulation. Although produced in large quantities on the island, none of it would stay there, but flowed off to foreign countries in a steady stream. The common explanation of this phenomenon was, that gold had become the cheapest thing the island produced, and was, therefore, the first thing exported. But a majority of those who said and heard this did not clearly see that the av-

erage purchasing power of gold the world over had not varied
in any degree; but that the price of almost every other thing
produced on the island had so varied and relatively increased,
by reason of domestic fiscal circumstances, that it was far better for the foreigner to take pay in gold for all the commodities he sold to the island, and then, with this gold, purchase in
other countries the very things which the island specially produced and wanted to sell. As already intimated, the islanders found great difficulty in understanding this little arrangement; but the foreigners understood it as by intuition, and
never failed to act upon it.*   All of this further contributed
to turn upside down and inside out the industries of the isl-
and; and while the Friends of Humanity continued to loudly
proclaim that the issue of more money would cure all difficulties, the people, sorely distressed, and ready to accept relief
from any quarter, began to loudly murmur, in turn, at what
seemed an unnecessary delay in making the issue; the fact
being, that although public opinion was nearly unanimous on
the subject, the regular time for the Congress of the island to
meet and enact the laws had not come round.

At last, the long-expected day arrived, and Congress assembled. All the special and immediate Friends of " More Money," of " Ideal Money," and of " Humanity," were members;
and hardly had the presiding officer taken his seat before fifty
men sprung for the floor, each with a resolution demanding
immediate fiscal legislation. The first resolution adopted was,
that the Government should at once supply all the money

---

* Whatever may have been the immediate effect of the gold-discoveries
in California and Australia, no economist of repute now holds to the opinion that the average purchasing power of gold all the world over is any
less than it was in 1849–'50; or, in other words, that any increase in the
quantity of gold since 1849–'50 has resulted in any present depreciation.

INCREASING THE VOLUME OF THE CURRENCY.

Capital. "By dividing this one dollar it becomes two, which makes more money. I pay
you these 'two dollars' for wages, you see."

Labor. "But when I go to buy bread I find them only worth one; so I don't see it."

which the wants of every body, and every trade and industry,
might, could, would, or should require; and that the money
thus issued should be a legal tender for the payment of all
debts, past, present, and prospective.

The next important question was, In what manner should

the new and unlimited supply of money be distributed? All saw at once that it would never do to commence on a system of giving unlimited something for unlimited nothing; and yet, if this was not done, how was it possible for the wants of those who had nothing, and who, of course, wanted money for this reason most imperatively, to be supplied? Besides, to create an unlimited supply of the new money, it would be necessary to have a good many hundreds of thousands of slips of paper with the words, " This is a dollar," " This is ten dollars," or " This is—" (some other amount), properly and artistically printed on them; all of which, in turn, would require a great expenditure, not only of ink and paper, but also of time; while the necessity of the hour was for immediate relief, especially to trade. It was therefore decided to leave the troublesome question of equal distribution for a time unsettled, and endeavor to first relieve trade by doubling the volume of the currency. And in order to do this at once, and without cost to the Government for engraving, printing, paper, and ink, it was therefore enacted that every one having legal-tender currency might cut or divide the same into two equal halves or pieces, and that each of these halves or pieces so resulting should be a legal tender to the full amount that the whole had previously been. At first thought, this proposition to exclude all those who had no money from participation in the new supply seemed most palpably unfair and unjust, but a little consideration satisfied to the contrary; for unless it was proposed to give away the new money, it was obvious that those only would get it who had money, and that the proportion which all such would obtain would be in proportion to what money they already had. It was, therefore, deemed wise to anticipate what was certain to be the ultimate result, and distribute it in the manner indicated.

CHAPTER XII.

GETTING SOBER.

IT was expected that this new and immense volume of currency, poured at once on to the wheels of trade, would immediately start the wheels. But, somehow, it didn't seem to have that effect at all. The wheels not only would not revolve, but the friction on them seemed to have become more persistent and chronic than ever. In fact, the doubling the volume of the currency, instead of increasing the before existing instrumentalities for facilitating exchanges, had really diminished them; for all who were willing to exchange commodities for the new currency either doubled the price of their commodities, or gave only half the quantity for what they regarded as half of the former money; so that with all this class the abundance of currency was relatively the same as before. But the majority who had any thing to sell would not accept the ideal money in exchange at all. They did not claim, they said, to be financiers, or philosophers, or even special friends of humanity; but they did think that they were not such fools that they could be made to believe that the half of a thing was equal to the whole, or that one bushel of grain could be converted into two by putting one bushel into two half-bushel measures.

The only really positive effect of the doubling of the volume of the currency in the manner authorized by law was, therefore, to scale all debts to the extent of fifty per cent., and in such a manner that creditors were wholly unable to help themselves; for by terms of the act every one dollar of old legal tender was now made two for all new legal-tender purposes. In this way the people on the island soon learned a most important elementary lesson in finance, which was, that the only one attribute of legal tender which is imperative and unavoidable* is its inherent power of canceling or liquidating debts or of tapping creditors—and this, too, irrespective of the endowment of the legal tender with any real or representative value. So that a truthful designation of the act in question would have been "An act to relieve debtors from half of their obligations, and swindle creditors to a corresponding extent of what was due them by the debtor's acknowledgment."

To the credit of the people of the island it must be recorded that, as a general rule, they were too honorable to take advantage of the law to do so wrong and mean a thing;† but the knowledge that every debtor had it in his power to so act,

---

* This is the American interpretation. The English interpretation of "legal tender" was brought out in a debate in the House of Lords, in June, 1811, when it was shown to mean, in its application to Great Britain, no more than this: that in a suit between creditor and debtor, if a judgment went against the debtor, he was allowed to plead a tender of bank-notes in arrest of execution, but he could not claim that the notes should be forced upon the creditor in discharge of the debt. During the long suspension of specie payments in Great Britain, therefore, bank-notes were never made legal tender in the American sense.

† After the Revolutionary war it was considered disgraceful to take advantage of the legal-tender character of the depreciated Continental or State paper money to liquidate debts with it; and the Society of Cincinnati expelled a member for so doing. The State of Rhode Island also, which longer than any of the other States endeavored to maintain by law the legal-tender character and use of such money, was often spoken of in consequence as "Rogue's" in place of "Rhode" Island.

and the fear that some would take advantage of their unquestionable legal privileges, contributed still further to bring all business to a stand-still.

There was also a curious phenomenon incident to the situation, and pertaining to the rate of interest, which excited no little comment and attention. Every body took it for granted that with an unlimited supply of money a low rate of interest would prevail, and that, however much the financiers and philosophers might disagree about other things, this one result would be certain. An eminently practical man in one of the public debating societies of the island thought he had definitely, and for all time, settled the question by authoritatively remarking that "an abundance of money does produce enterprise, prosperity, and progress;" "that when money was plenty interest would be lower," just as when horses and hogs are abundant, horses and hogs would be cheap. He, for one, "put aside all these old theories, these platitudes of finance." There was "no vitality in them." He preferred "to take the actual results, and the actual condition of the country, and let theory go to the dogs."*

There was so much of originality and home sense in these remarks, so much of a lordly contemning of the teachings of musty old experience, that the friends of the orator thought him much more worthy than ever of the executive chair formerly filled by the wise Robinson Crusoe. But, unfortunately for the orator, he hadn't got far enough along in his financial primer to appreciate the difference between capital and currency; and in the simplicity of his heart imagined that it was

---

* To any who may desire to know how far imagination has been drawn upon for this picture, reference is made to the speech of Hon. O. P. Morton, United States Senate, "Congressional Record," vol. ii., part i., Forty-third Congress, First Session, p. 669.

all the same, whether we had pictures of horses, hogs, and money, or real horses, hogs, and money, which represent and are accumulated by labor.   So the things which he thus settled in opposition to theory and experience wouldn't stay settled; and the islanders in due time came to a realizing sense of the following truths: that the more of a redundant, irredeemable paper that is issued, the more it depreciates, and the more it is depreciated, the more there is required of it to transact business; and that if any one borrows depreciated money to do any thing, he has to borrow a greater nominal amount than he would of money that was not depreciated; and that it is on *the number* of nominal dollars, and *not on their purchasing power*, that the rate of interest is always calculated.   The invariable rise in prices consequent on the depreciation of money (price as already explained being the purchasing power of any commodity or service expressed in money), furthermore stimulates borrowing for the purpose of speculation; and the more borrowers, the more competition; and the more the competition to obtain an article or service, the higher the price demanded for it.

Again, the currency of the island having been made artificially abundant, its exchangeable value was always uncertain; and capital, therefore, as it always does at such times, locked up its pockets, hesitated to take risks, and, if it consented to loan at all, demanded extra pay by reason of the increased risk or induced scarcity.*

---

* The pertinacity with which a mind befogged on the subject of money and currency holds on to the delusion that the making and issue of promises to pay, and calling the same money, is equivalent to the creation of wealth; and, *vice versâ*, that the cancellation or withdrawal, by payment, of such promises is the same thing as the destruction of wealth, and also tends to make money—in the sense of capital—scarce, and interest high,

After testing all these principles experimentally for a considerable time, the people on the island came to see that the

---

finds many amusing illustrations, which for educational purposes are better than arguments.

For example, we have, first, the assumption of a leading Senator of the United States (already referred to, and which, if not on record, would seem incredible) that because an increased supply of horses and hogs made available to a market make horses and hogs cheap, therefore an increased supply of evidences that capital had been borrowed, used, and never paid, would tend to increase the quantity and rate of interest of loanable capital. A corresponding illustration is also to be found in the case of the member of the Continental Congress mentioned by Pelatiah Webster, who, when the subject of increased taxation for the support of the war was under consideration, indignantly asked "if he was expected to help tax the people, when they could go to the printing-office and get money by the cart-load ?"

The experience of the Irish mob also finds an appropriate place under this head, which made a bonfire of all the notes issued by an obnoxious private banker that they could gather, little imagining, as they shouted and capered with wild delight about the fire that consumed them, that, in place of impoverishing, they were really enriching, their enemy.

The following story, also illustrative of the same popular fallacy, passes current in one of the towns of Eastern Connecticut: During the severe financial panic of 1857, an honest country farmer and deacon, who, by virtue of being a considerable stockholder in one of the local banks, had been placed as a figure-head on its board of directors, was applied to by a farmer friend to help him in procuring from the bank a small loan. Knowing that the times were hard, and money scarce, the deacon, although desirous of obliging his friend, did not at once commit himself, but promised to go to the bank, and make his action contingent upon the state of affairs which he might there find. The two friends, accordingly, went into town the next day (which happened to be the culminating day of the crisis, when every promise to pay issued by any bank was, in the general distrust, gathered up and rushed in for redemption); and, while the applicant for the loan waited outside, the director entered the bank to reconnoitre. Passing into the directors' room, and thence behind the counter, he said little, but, keeping

possession of money was the consequence rather than the
cause of wealth; and that, except under special circumstances
and conditions, the rate of interest depends on the abundance
or scarcity of that part of the capital of a community which
does not consist of money; and that it can not be permanently lowered by any increase in the quantity of money.*

In this way, through the school of hard experience, the people on the island came gradually to understand that there
were certain economic truths which had got to be accepted
and lived up to in order to insure either individual or national prosperity. They came to understand that property is a

his eyes wide open, did not fail to notice the extraordinarily large packages of bills, filling safe and drawers, which, to the annoyance and strain
of the bank, had been recently sent in for payment. Seeking no further
proof of the financial strength of his institution, he returned to the street,
and, informing his friend that every thing was all right, the latter next
entered, and confidently asked for his discount. To his great surprise, he
received the usual polite answer, that "they would be too glad to oblige
him, but that, really, they had no money." "Out of money!" said the deacon, when the result of the application was made known to him. "Out of
money! How can they lie so, when I have just seen the safe and drawers full of it? As a Christian man, and an officer of the church, I can't
conscientiously be a director and stockholder any longer in such an im-
moral institution." And yet, if, on returning home, the good deacon had
found in his table-drawer a number of his individual promissory-notes,
signed and ready to issue, but not issued, he would not have thought himself any richer by their existence, but, on the contrary, would have felt
much more comfortable at such a time to know that the notes were all under double-lock security, or, better, if he saw them vanishing into ashes.
And yet, in the case of the bank-notes, he couldn't understand why they
were not money, to be used at all times and under all circumstances!

* Between the years 1860 and 1870, the United States doubled the quantity of currency available for use by its citizens, and yet the rate of interest was as high in the latter year as in the former.

physical actuality, the result of some form of labor; that capital is that portion of the results of production which can be reserved and made available for new and further production; that money is an instrumentality for facilitating the distribution and use of capital and the interchange of products and services; that production alone buys production; that when one buys goods with a paper representative or symbol of money, the goods are not paid for until the representative is substituted by a value of some sort in labor, or money, or some other commodity; and, finally, that a country and its inhabitants increase in wealth or abundance by increasing their products, rather than by inordinately multiplying machinery for the exchange of products. They also saw that the promises to pay which they had been using and regarding as money were debts; and that debts, as well as all other forms of title, are but shadows of the property they represent; and that, in endeavoring to all get rich by first creating debts, then calling the debts money, and the money wealth, they had been led, successively, into speculation, extravagance, idleness, and impoverishment; and, like the dog in the fable, which let go of the meat in crossing a stream for the sake of grasping its shadow, they had lost much of real wealth resulting from previous industry by trying to make the shadow of wealth supply the place of its substance.

Coming to gradually realize, also, that one of the first requisites for an increase of trade was that confidence should exist between the buyer and the seller, but that such confidence never would exist so long as the representatives of value, or other intermediate agencies made use of for facilitating exchanges, were of an uncertain, fluctuating character, they also came finally to the conclusion that there was no economy in using cheap money; or, in other words, that the loss and waste in-

THE HUNGRY DOG AND THE SHADOW.
Grasp at the Shadow and lose the Substance.

evitably resulting from the use of poor tools (money being a
tool) was many times in excess of the interest accruing from
any increased cost of good tools. So reasoning, gold, or un-
doubted promises to pay gold, gradually came once more into
use as money on the island.

There were some prophecies, and a good deal of apprehension, that there would be difficulty experienced in obtaining sufficient gold to serve as money or as a basis for currency, especially when it was remembered that the influence of all that had recently happened had been to encourage the export of all the gold that was owned or produced on the island. But as the goldsmiths and the jewelers never experienced any difficulty during the war with the cannibals, or afterward, in obtaining all the gold they wanted, no matter how scarce and valuable it was as compared with currency, and could have had a hundred times more than they actually used, if their customers had been willing to pay for it; so the merchants, traders, and people at large on the island, as soon as they became satisfied that it was economical to use gold, and determined to have it, experienced no difficulty in obtaining an ample supply.

One circumstance which, pending this result, tended to greatly relieve the popular apprehension on this score, was the reading in foreign newspapers that the people in certain comparatively poor countries — as Oregon, Arizona, Nevada, and Washington Territory—had no more difficulty in obtaining and retaining all the gold that they found it desirable to use for the purpose of money, than they had in obtaining and retaining all the wheelbarrows and steam-engines that they desired to use in conducting their business; and laughed when any body talked of depriving them of their gold money.

The first step having been thus taken in the right direction, a sequence of other proper acts occurred as naturally and with the same favorable results as in the celebrated case of the old woman and the kid; in which it will be remembered that as soon as the water began to quench the fire, the fire

began to burn the stick, the stick began to beat the dog, the
dog began to bite the kid, and, as a consequence of this sequence and its concluding act, the old woman got safely home
with the kid, though at a period of the evening much later
than was desirable or proper. And so, by a succession of
events, prosperity slowly but surely came back to the island.

As for the Friends of Humanity, who had been the authors
of so much financial and commercial disturbance and national
misfortune, they soon ceased to command attention from any
one, then became objects of laughter and derision, and finally
passed out of the remembrance of the people, who were now
all too busy in restoring their fortunes to give a thought to by-
gone and mortifying experiences. Some became convinced
of their errors, and made good citizens; but in the case of
the majority, the belief that the calling of things of no intrinsic value by the name of money was equivalent to the creation
of wealth, became chronic, and finally developed into a harm-
less insanity. On pleasant days they might often be seen on
the corners of the streets gathering leaves and bits of sticks and
straws, and telling the children that assembled about them
that all that was necessary to make these worthless gatherings
money was to simply have confidence that they were so. But
this was asking for a simplicity of belief that was a little too
much, even for the children.

It only remains to add that, as memorials of this eventful
history, there is still exhibited in one of the public buildings
on the island an exact model of the cave in which the vener-
able Robinson Crusoe dwelt, and, what is even more interesting, the identical chest which he brought from the ship, and
which contained the pins, needles, knives, cloth, and scissors,
and the three great bags of what was then useless, but now

good and true, money. Numerous specimens of the "ideal
money" may also be seen in the same room, together with a
picture of the barber who papered his shop with it, and of the
dog which the people paraded in the streets covered with a
plaster of pitch and currency.*

---

* Such were some of the uses finally made of the Continental currency.
See Sumner's "History of American Currency," p. 46.